DADDY
are you sad?

ISBN: 978-1-941213-03-2

Cover design: Gavin Miles and Teresa Sommers
Text layout design: Kristi Yoder

Printed in the USA

For more information about Christian Aid Ministries, see page 247.

Published by:
TGS International
P.O. Box 355
Berlin, Ohio 44610 USA
Phone: 330-893-4828
Fax: 330-893-2305
www.tgsinternational.com

TGS000795

LILY A. BEAR

DADDY
are you sad?

*A shattering health diagnosis
and haunting questions.
Where would this journey
lead the young family?*

Dedicated to

Dallas and Dustin

whose father left them a legacy of faith in God.

Preface

In this heartrending, yet uplifting, story, Donny and Nicole Good fulfill the mission God calls them to. As Donny battles leukemia, they face fear, anger, and discouragement, but are repeatedly drawn back to the love of their heavenly Father.

Donny kept a personal journal and also corresponded extensively by email with his wide circle of friends. Praise God for nudging him to do so! These meticulous writings provide a clear picture of his journey, both physically and spiritually. Much of the text of this book comes directly from his writings.

During his battle with leukemia, Donny interacted with many people, both in America and Mexico. In faithful obedience to his heavenly Father, Donny utilized every opportunity to serve his fellowmen. He offered friendship while sharing the good news of God's love and salvation. Forgetting his own problems, he showed others where to find peace in the midst of their suffering.

As I became involved in this project, I faced this question: *Would I be able to surrender to God if He asked me to go through something as hard as what Donny did?* I shrank at the implications.

I faced another question as well. *How could I write about Donny's incredible witness for God without Satan attacking me?* Then it became clear to me. God is omnipresent and omnipotent. God's mercy and grace are always available, and His presence is constant. God is always good!

But He asks for surrender. He wants everything: our hearts, our minds, and our bodies. We find rest as we put our lives in God's keeping. Donny did, and we can too. I don't know my future. You don't know yours. But God does. May each of us submit our lives to God and allow them to have an impact for Him.

I have been touched by Donny's life of faithfulness, his strength, and his courage in the midst of affliction. May Donny's story also touch your life and inspire you to a closer walk with God.

—Lily A. Bear

Table of Contents

Introduction

As I walk through our clinic, the Hope4Cancer Institute in Tijuana, Mexico, I come to the newly constructed wing. On the wall I see imprinted in big, bold letters the words "Donny B. Good Wing." My heart wells up with emotion. Memories come flooding back of a young man, his wife, and their two young children. To this day, their fervent plea resounds in my heart, "We are in the midst of a living nightmare. Will you please help us?"

As I pause, I think of the significance of this new wing. Our biggest construction project in over a decade doubles our capacity and amplifies our ability to serve patients. You may wonder why I chose to name such an important part of the cancer clinic after one of its patients. Read on, and I hope you will understand why.

Many of God's children come to us, stay with us for a few weeks, and leave our clinic with a renewed sense of hope. Many of them experience miraculous recoveries after long and steady battles. These victories do not happen without God's divine grace and the relentless work of a committed and dedicated staff. However, in our defeats we are also reminded every day, very often in harsh terms, about the destructive reality of cancer. The complexity and aggressiveness of some cases leave us with seemingly unbeatable odds despite our best efforts.

Hope4Cancer Institute, in many ways, is a place where hope and despair clash in a relentless war against attrition. Standing in the maelstrom of it all over the past twenty-three years, I can tell you that the crisis of this disease can rip open a person as nothing else can, revealing the human spirit within. When you squeeze an orange, all you get is orange juice. What is inside is revealed.

A few patients and their devoted companions left indelible marks on my life. They demonstrated to me the power of their spirit in the way they bravely faced their trials and tribulations. They showed unshakable faith against insurmountable odds. Even as I attempted to bring healing to them, they in turn strengthened my spirit. They blessed me in many ways and became a part of my life.

A shining star among these was my remarkable patient and friend, Donny B. Good. Frankly, I could not think of anybody better who would honor Hope4Cancer Institute with his name imprinted on its walls.

Donny was a mere twenty-five years old when he was diagnosed with acute myelogenous leukemia. The disease was presented to him as a death sentence. The negative side effects of chemotherapy worsened his condition to the point where he was given only weeks to live. Donny came to us weak, tired, and, without a doubt, gravely ill. Unlike most patients who typically stay with us for two to three weeks and continue their therapy at home, Donny stayed with us for over five months, since he required constant monitoring. But while he was physically and probably mentally fragile, he was spiritually strong and in tune with the Holy Spirit. In the face of his challenges, we saw revealed before us the Spirit-led person that he truly was.

Think about it. Donny had everything to lose. He faced the prospect of leaving behind his young wife and children, aged two and four, and the prospect of his family unit being derailed before it had even gotten very far on the tracks! Donny faced these realities daily along with the fear, despair, and pain that they brought.

Yet Donny tried to replace his fears with his undying faith in his one, true God. Easier said than done, even for all of us healthier ones, isn't it? The guiding principle that allowed him to do this was his understanding of the God-given purpose for his life. Putting God first gave him the ability to see past his circumstances and focus on what was important.

Donny fought for his family with tremendous passion. He wanted to continue living, to be there for them, to serve them. He wanted to be the devoted husband, the caring father, the dutiful son. To win the battle, he took on the most rigorous of our therapies with a level of gusto that I had never seen before in any of my patients. For example, he is the only patient who ever consumed a daily dose of seventy-two enzyme pills—the maximum possible dose that an individual can tolerate.

Donny lived almost another six months after making the courageous choice to embrace our natural therapies at Hope4Cancer Institute. He experienced a much better-than-expected quality of life before he finally left us to be with the Lord. Those six months were well beyond even my medical expectations, given the seriousness of his condition.

Donny was not merely a patient or a friend; he was far more than that. In many ways, he uplifted me even as I tried to do the same for him. This others-focused nature of his behavior extended to his fellow patients. In the moments of camaraderie during breaks between therapies or in the evenings, he would minister to them in a loving, nonintrusive way. This beautiful balance in his personality is something I remember vividly every time I think of him.

You may wonder, "What does the B stand for in Donny's name?" Because Donny could not use his middle initial, H, in his email address, he chose to use B as a reminder to himself to be good—to embrace to the fullest each day of life granted to him. It also became a pet name between us. When he would leave after an appointment, I would remind him, "Donny, now be good!"

In many ways, Donny connected to my soul from the very first day I met him, reminding me of all the values I personally hold dear in my life. I can only wish he were still with us today, but God's plans for him were different. He will live on with us through this amazing chronicle, a project his wife Nicole has undertaken. Instead of wallowing in the pain of his loss, Nicole has chosen to celebrate his life in a truly significant way.

His spirit undoubtedly lives on in the family he has left behind. Nicole has made the decision to grow stronger in his physical absence by remembering his spiritual strength. I hope and pray every person suffering from cancer takes the time to read this chronicle and be uplifted by it. Although this is not the typical "success" story of life overcoming death, I personally believe that in his passing, Donny has achieved a victory of the spirit that is a lesson for every person reading this book, whether or not he is fighting cancer.

—Antonio Jimenez, M.D. (Dr. Tony)

1

Shattering Diagnosis

I cy wind swept across the parking lot as Nicole Good tucked her gloved hand into her husband's. Donny squeezed her fingers. They both wished they could have stayed in Oregon where "winter coats" were either a light rain jacket or a heavy sweater. The two-week Christmas vacation with Nicole's family there had been wonderful for both her and four-month-old Dallas, but Donny's anticipation of ridding himself of his recurring flu-like symptoms in the warmer climate had not materialized. In fact, now that they were back in Ohio, he felt more ill than before they had left for Oregon.

Today I will find out what is plaguing me! It is high time to get to the root of this tiredness! With these hopeful thoughts Donny mustered extra energy to firmly climb the steps to the chiropractic office where he had recently had blood work done.

Warm air enveloped the family as they entered Doctor Jones's office, but the cold fingers of fear around Nicole's heart refused to leave. *Lord, I am so fearful.* Numbly the young mother took a seat and removed Dallas's cap. *I can't even pray my fears away! I am so afraid Dr. Jones found something serious through the blood work. Please, Lord, let it be something simple!*

Yet one look at Dr. Jones's somber face as he entered the consulting room sent her heart plummeting. *Something is wrong! Something is seriously wrong!* The tentacles of fear twisted tighter, cutting off her air until Nicole thought she would faint. Her heart screamed in protest. *God, I don't want to know! I'm so scared!*

For almost a year, Nicole had been plagued with a nagging feeling that something terrible would happen to her husband. Today it seemed that her fears were becoming reality.

"I need to get the results of your blood work," Dr. Jones quietly informed the Goods as he walked from the room into his private office. Unknown to Donny and Nicole, he found it extremely difficult to give them this report. Entering his office, Dr. Jones shut the door and bowed his head. "Lord, how can I face this young couple? Help me. I can't do it on my own strength. Bless them, Lord, and give them guidance for this hard, hard road."

Agitation filled Nicole as they waited for the doctor's return. Her mind replayed some of the things her husband had shared with her. She remembered the fear that had gripped her then.

"I feel so unsettled!" Donny had stated one evening. "It seems God is telling me He has more for me than just going to work every day. I feel God has some other kind of work waiting. Nicole darling, we must earnestly pray."

"What do you mean?" she had asked, not wanting to accept the implications of his thoughts. "All men go to work."

What had worried her most was the far-away look that came over his face before he had replied, "Yes, but I know God has something He wants me to do for Him." From then on her husband had prayed daily, "God, we are submitted and open to whatever you want to do with us."

Why do I have to remember my husband's prayers now? Nicole asked herself as she waited. They reminded her of a choice that continued to confront her—a choice she did not want to face. Would she hold onto these fears, or would she submit to God? She found her heart crying out against submission because she was so afraid God would ask something sacrificial of her, something hard!

Nicole tried to push the tormenting thoughts away. She didn't want to think them. She wanted her husband to be strong and healthy. She wanted to spend the rest of her life with him. *Lord, I don't want you to give us something hard to do! I can't handle this! I want to get up and go home. I don't want to be sitting here in this stifling room! I want everything to be normal.*

But things were not normal. Dr. Jones was entering the room. Nicole's hands shook, her heart pounded, and nauseating fear pulsed through her.

"Donny," Dr. Jones began. He took a deep breath and

began again. "Donny, we have the results of your blood work. We have found high amounts of abnormal cells in your blood. It appears, Donny, that you have acute myelogenous leukemia, a cancer of the white blood cells. I am trying to get you into the Columbus James Cancer Institute tomorrow. We need to do something immediately."

Leukemia! Nicole felt as though she were being sucked into a bottomless vortex.

Leukemia! Donny sat stunned at the shocking diagnosis. *Not leukemia! I've been married only three years. I have a four-month-old baby boy. And my wife! Lord, no! No. This can't be happening. Not cancer. I'm only twenty-five!* Shock waves pulsed through his body, but he willed himself to listen, to make sense of Dr. Jones's words.

Surely I haven't heard right. His mind felt jumbled. *I must focus! If only I can get past my dizziness, I will be able to clear up this misunderstanding. There has to be a mistake! Surely there is something more to this, a bright side to this awful report.*

But instead of giving them reassuring words, Dr. Jones walked over to them. Reaching out his hands, he laid one on Donny's shoulder and one on Nicole's.

"May I pray with you?" he asked, gently breaking into Donny's tumultuous thoughts.

In the midst of Donny's shock and confusion, he felt compassion radiating through Dr. Jones's warm hand. As he looked up into the doctor's eyes, he saw his own pain mirrored in them. Numbly Donny nodded and bowed his head. He gripped Nicole's icy hand and felt her shaking all over.

"God, we come to you. We ask for strength for this young couple and for grace for the trial they are facing. God, our God . . ." Their chiropractor's professional voice broke as he tried to control his emotions. Then it hit Donny fully. *Cancer. Cancer! Isn't cancer a death sentence?*

Donny's mind skipped back in time. *Is this the reason I've been so tired and dizzy for the last two months? All that nausea and pain . . . Maybe this is why I've been falling asleep on the job? Oh, God, let the test results be wrong!* his heart cried out. Yet somehow he knew they weren't. For the last month he had tried to convince himself nothing was wrong. He had tried to blame his symptoms on too little sleep or the many changes confronting them as a young-married couple.

I have responsibilities! I am a husband and a father, he had kept reminding himself. *I've lifted weights for years. I weigh two hundred pounds. I operate a bulldozer. Am I not supposed to be the strong person taking care of my family?*

Then he thought of his wife's fears and the conversation they had had a month earlier. He had tried to downplay his tiredness and his weight loss. "Sweetheart, I work long days and I'm director of the church chorus," he had told her as he had tried to put her fears to rest. "Both jobs take a lot of energy. Besides, we have a colicky baby who doesn't let me sleep through the night." But he felt guilty as he thought of the times lately that he had dumped his lunch so Nicole wouldn't find out he was feeling too nauseated to eat.

Donny's mind jumped back to the present. *What have I missed of Dr. Jones's prayer?* he wondered. It was hard to stay focused. It seemed as if this wasn't real. *Is this a nightmare? Will I soon wake up and find it over?* Little Dallas whimpered, and reality returned. *God!* the young father's heart cried out. *Not cancer! My wife! My little boy! No. It can't be.*

While Donny was struggling with the doctor's verdict, Nicole felt comforted and overwhelmed by their doctor's passionate prayer. She heard Dr. Jones taking deep breaths. Seeing his tear-filled eyes, she realized, *He doesn't want to be giving us this devastating news. This is incredibly hard on him. He truly does care about us.* For a few seconds Nicole felt wrapped in warmth, but it was quickly replaced by paralyzing fear.

Her face turned ashen as she grabbed hold of her husband's arm. She felt herself slipping into shock as her fears closed in on her. Donny tried to support his wife, but it seemed as if his own strength was being drained away by the agony gripping his heart. He could hardly bear to watch his wife's big blue eyes darken into pools of grief. Would she make it to the car without fainting? How could he help her when he hardly had the strength to carry Dallas?

Help us, Lord, help us, he pleaded inwardly when Nicole

slumped forward, unable to climb into the car alone. God answered, giving him strength to help her in. When Donny closed the car door, a dam broke loose, and Nicole burst out crying in great gulping sobs, "Why, God? Why? Why? Why?"

Donny felt too devastated to comfort his wife. He needed someone to comfort him. But who? His parents had just left for a stay of several months in Florida. His only brother lived in Oklahoma. His in-laws and Nicole's twin sister Michelle and her husband, Gail Bear, all lived in Oregon. "Lord, is there no one for us? Have you left us all alone?" he cried.

"Donny, let's go to Tillman and Elaine!" Nicole sobbed. "We have to go to Tillman and Elaine now! Gail and Michelle would want us to go to his parents. Sweetheart! Please! Let's go to Gail's parents," she kept repeating, until her frantic words penetrated Donny's fogginess, and he felt his mind clear. Of course. Nicole was right. God was giving him direction through the words of his wife. What comfort! God had not left them alone. He had someone for them.

"Yes, honey, we'll go to Tillman and Elaine," Donny said, reaching over and touching her arm. It tore his heart to hear her weep. Yet he could do nothing to take away her tears or her fears.

But yes, Tillman and Elaine were just who they needed. Thinking about his brother-in-law's parents sidetracked him for a bit. It also flooded his mind with happier memories—memories of when he and Nicole announced their own engagement at the end of Gail and Michelle's wedding reception.

Their engagement. A faint smile tugged at Donny's mouth as the memories of Proposal Rock popped into his mind. He thought of the day over three years ago when he had found a picture of the place and exclaimed to his empty room, "It's perfect! I've found the perfect spot to propose to my sweetheart!" He was in Ohio at the time, far from the Oregon coast where he hoped to propose. Nicole, far away in Oregon, knew nothing of his plan to ask her to marry him.

Donny remembered his indecision before reaching that point. He had sought God's direction before even beginning a relationship with Nicole and then throughout their courtship. Prayer was an integral part of his life, and he had earnestly prayed as he weighed the issue of marriage. As he had prayed, he had felt God's blessing on his decision to ask Nicole to share life with him. When he saw the picture of the rock, he had been contemplating when and where to ask the life-changing question.

Donny's smile grew as visions of the Oregon coast took his mind off his shattering diagnosis, and he reminisced of happier times. As they drove west through the city of Lima, he did not notice the traffic lights or businesses. Instead he was hearing the thundering waves crashing around famous Proposal Rock before they rolled onto the sandy beach. He was seeing himself standing with

Nicole, the two of them mesmerized by a flaming sunset stretching on and on across the water.

"Are you going to call? Donny! We need to call Tillman!" his wife's panicky voice jerked him back to reality. The stark facts stared him in the face again.

"Yes," Donny assured her, reaching for his phone.

"Tillman, it's Donny. May we stop in? We just left Dr. Jones's office, and it's bad. It's really bad." As he choked out the words, their devastating implications returned with a vengeance.

When the young couple got out of their car, Tillman was waiting with open arms of love and comfort for Donny. Nicole watched her husband literally walk into Tillman's arms. The men wept together as Donny sobbed, "It's cancer. I have an acute cancer of the blood." Elaine hugged Nicole, and together the four of them wept.

The grieving couple could not bring themselves to leave the Bears' home and the oasis it provided. Warm comfort blanketed Nicole when Elaine draped an afghan over her and nursing Dallas. Donny gathered his courage and shared with Tillman his desire to be anointed with oil.

"Tillman, Dr. Jones said he hoped I will be able to go to Columbus to begin treatment tomorrow. I feel the need to have an anointing service first. God gives us instructions on being anointed with oil, and I want to let God have His perfect will in my life. When we were in Oregon a few weeks ago, I first thought of it as something I should do. What do you think?"

"You definitely have my blessing. Let's call our bishop and see if we can arrange it for this evening," Tillman encouraged. "Would you want to hold the service here?" he asked. "Elaine is planning to feed you supper, so you may as well just have it here afterward."

"Thanks. I would like that. I don't know what we would do without your love and understanding," Donny answered shakily as he rested his head in his hands. "Could you call Brother John? I'm just not up to it."

"I'll be glad to," Tillman assured him as he reached for the phone and dialed. When John, their bishop, answered, Tillman explained Donny's situation and desire for anointing. A short time later it was arranged. The church ministry would come later in the evening for the anointing service. In the meantime, Donny and Nicole had other phone calls to make.

. . . .

When Wilmer and Miriam Good heard the devastating news in Florida, they wept on the phone, longing to put their arms around their suffering son and his family. Miriam felt a jolt like an electric shock course through her. Trembling with weakness, she fell into the nearest chair, thinking, *This can't be! Maybe the diagnosis is wrong. God in heaven, hold our dear children in your arms.*

"Donny, we haven't unpacked everything from the vehicle yet. We will repack and start home tomorrow." Wilmer's words of support made Donny and Nicole feel wrapped in love.

"Oh, honey, God spared our son when he was born," Miriam reminisced with her husband as she wiped persistent tears. "Remember the doctor telling us how fortunate we were not to have a brain-damaged baby when he had a bowel movement before birth and was born in toxic water?"

"Yes, I do," Wilmer replied. "God definitely answered our prayers when everything turned out all right. I had to think too of the time we were on our way to the emergency room when Donny could hardly breathe. How old was he? I seem to have lost track of time. Right now his whole short life seems to be flashing before me." Wilmer's heart constricted in pain. *Twenty-five years! Twenty-five short years!*

"Five months," Miriam replied. "He was five months old, and I was afraid he would take his last breath on the way to the hospital. But God touched him. Wilmer, God can touch and heal him again. We need to keep reminding ourselves that God is holding our son in His hands."

"But Miriam, we also need to surrender to whatever God wills," he reminded gently. "I, too, believe God can and will heal if it is His divine plan."

"That is what is so hard! Oh, honey. My heart breaks for Nicole and sweet baby Dallas! Why them? Nicole relies tremendously on Donny. As children, she and Michelle depended on each other for everything, and in their marriages they seem to have transferred that dependency to their husbands. What will Nicole do if Donny doesn't make it?" Miriam's sobs filled the room, but her husband knew she wasn't questioning God's supremacy; she was weeping because of her love for their son and his family and the pain they, too, were experiencing.

Wilmer recalled another time when God had spared their son's life. "Remember the tornado that roared through our area right after you and I got home from church? We were so worried because we didn't know if Donny was still at church or if he was out in the storm. I remember how he came bursting through the door soaking wet, his face pasty white, yet glowing because of God's miraculous protection."

"That's right. I had forgotten all about that!" Miriam reached for another hankie. "Donny said God must have sent an angel to keep him from harm because a tree landed on his car hood only inches from his face! Seven years ago. Seven short years since our son was eighteen." She paused for a bit, remembering. "There was still another time when God kept him safe. Remember the time he was riding his moped home from school when he was about fourteen? It was terribly windy, and the wind caught his bike, flipping him up in the air. All he ended up with was a four-inch gash on his shinbone! That makes four miracles, Wilmer."

"Four miracles that we know of," her husband replied with a smile. "It makes me wonder how many other times God protected him from serious harm."

As Donny made the telephone call to Oregon, Nicole's twin sister Michelle was dropping a kiss onto one-and-a-half-year-old Caleb's forehead before tucking his blanket up around his shoulders. "Precious darling," she murmured, "come summer, you will get a tiny playmate!" She patted her son as she dreamed of the coming event. *Won't it be lovely to have another dear little bundle to love and cuddle?!* Hearing the phone ring, she hurried to answer it as quickly as possible so that Caleb would not awaken.

"Michelle," Donny's urgent voice startled her. Her knees went weak when she heard him ask, "Where is Gail? Can you get him on the phone?"

Oh! What is Donny going to say? Does this call have anything to do with his constant tiredness when their family was here over Christmas? Michelle's thoughts grew anxious as she waited for her husband to turn on the speakerphone.

"Gail, I want you and Michelle to sit down. I have bad news. The test results I got today say I have a serious form of leukemia." Each word exploded like a bullet, sending shock waves through them. They stared at each other in stunned disbelief.

"Oh, dear God! No! No! No!" Michelle cried out in anguish for her twin sister and brother-in-law. She felt as if a knife were twisting inside her and as if she were the one suffering from horrible pain.

"Michelle and Gail, we need you to be strong." Her

sister's pleading, weeping voice sounded as if it was next door instead of two-thirds of the distance across the continent. "We can't do this alone. We need you! We are at Tillman's house and are getting ready to have an anointing service."

At least they are with Gail's parents, Michelle thought as she listened to Donny finish with, "We will call you in the morning. Just pray."

Both Gail and Michelle were in shock. Going over to the couch, they fell on their knees. No words came, only deep, agonizing pain as they put their arms around each other and cried to God for help and strength.

Nicole, my sister! Why my sister and her husband? Michelle silently rebelled at the seeming unfairness. Her mind replayed their preteen and teen years and how people had said it was impossible to separate them. Yes, they had certainly done everything together! She remembered going to piano practice when they were eleven. There they had met Mennonite girls who were also taking lessons. It was the first time they had ever met Mennonites. Both she and Nicole had been drawn to the girls and had gladly attended the Mennonite summer Bible school and an occasional church service when their parents allowed it.

Five years later, when Michelle and Nicole were sixteen, their parents had consented and the twins had become members of the Porter Mennonite Church. Then in the years that followed, both of them had married young men from a Mennonite church in Ohio.

Why this, God? Michelle continued to struggle. As she did, God gently reminded her of the words from Scripture, "Whom I love, I will chasten." She remembered God's mercies in the past, and slowly she found rest in knowing God was in control of Donny and Nicole's lives. Even greater comfort filled her as she thought of God's promise that He would not give His children more than they could bear.

. . . .

Nicole's parents, Floyd and Dee Smallfoot, were both at home that memorable evening when Donny shared the test results. Dee had just gotten home from work when she answered the ringing telephone to hear Donny ask, "Is Dad there? I have something to tell you both. Could you put the speakerphone on?"

Dee held her breath. The message coming through the phone was overwhelming. All she could say was, "Oh, no . . . no. Please God, no!" as she clung to Floyd.

"We love you, Donny, very much," Floyd and Dee sobbed together into the phone. "We care about you, and we will be praying for you."

"I love you too, Mom and Dad," Donny assured them before hanging up.

Dee's thoughts turned back to the days the family had spent together at Christmas. She had prepared for weeks for the arrival of their children and grandchildren. After Donny, Nicole, and Dallas had been with them several days, she had realized that Donny was not feeling well. She had noticed he didn't have any color in his lips. Donny had tried so hard to be upbeat. He had kept trying different things to help what he thought were gall bladder problems.

This had worried Dee, and before Donny and Nicole had left for Ohio, she had encouraged him, "Please, Donny, see a doctor when you get home."

Now she wept aloud as her heart cried, *Oh, God, I did not expect this. Donny is a lighthouse of your love shining through him! Isn't it wrong that he should have to suffer?*

Floyd and Dee called their pastor and his wife, who came over right away to give them support and pray with them. Before leaving, Pastor Herd shared the comforting thought from Romans 8 that God never allows pain in the lives of His children without a purpose. God never allows Satan, or circumstances, or any ill-intended person to afflict us unless He uses that affliction for our good. God never wastes pain. He always causes it to work for our ultimate good with the goal of conforming us more into the likeness of His Son.

. . . .

Keep a journal. Keep a journal. When the inner command refused to be quiet, Donny sorted through his desk that evening until he found an unused school tablet. He picked up a pen and wrote this, the first entry in what became his tablet journal.

January 12, 2006 – It was in the back of my mind when I was in Oregon to request anointing with oil when I got home. So I was somewhat prepared for this.

"Would you share your testimony?" the ministers asked me.

"I have peace with God, and my body is His to do with as He wills," I answered.

My testimony was more to me than just words. These were the feelings of my heart and echoed the prayer of submission and openness I had been praying for over a year. I wanted to do whatever God wanted.

After completing the journal entry, Donny sat lost in thought as he contemplated his anointing service. All three ministers had been present as Bishop John Brunk led out. How had John said it? "Anointing with oil is a divine suggestion. It is an outward symbol of the presence of the Holy Spirit and an action we take to encourage our faith. When we pray the prayer of faith, we are opening and surrendering ourselves completely to whatever God has in store for us. As our brother said in his testimony, we give God ourselves 'to do with as He wills.' The prayer of faith should be an expression of the whole life. Jesus Christ is concerned about the welfare of the whole person—spirit, soul, and body."

Yes, God's presence had definitely been felt! Did the three ministers know the profound love he experienced as they laid their hands on his head and prayed for him?

Did they guess the peace that had washed over him when Bishop John touched his forehead with oil? He had prayed the prayer of faith—faith to accept being healed or not. Yet his heart's longing was, *Lord, let it be healing.*

Many prayers ascended for the young couple as night settled over the country. The wife of a minister who had been at the anointing service wept as she told her husband, "I don't think I will ever forget Donny's chalk-white face or the way Nicole laid her head on my shoulder. She felt like a limp rag! My heart is bleeding for them."

Though Donny had partaken of sweet fellowship with God during the anointing service, as night fell it seemed that the devil was bent on destroying his peace. Instead of falling into a peaceful sleep that January 12 night, the wakeful hours became filled with doubts until utter agony engulfed him. Night's darkness pressed in from the outside, worming its way into Donny's soul.

Nicole faced her own battle. *Will I wake up and find my husband gone?* she repeatedly asked herself. She felt the vortex of blackness swirling around her, trying to pull her into its dark, bottomless hole.

God, why are you doing this to us? Her tortured cry was inaudible. Instead of speaking aloud, she held tighter to the hand covering hers. *Oh, Lord, we are too young!* She lay in bed battling her fears, her four-month-old baby on the one side of her and the love of her life on the other. Sheer exhaustion caused her to drift off to sleep, but she would jerk awake to ask, "Darling, are you all right?"

"Yes, sweetheart, I'm fine." Her husband would whisper, knowing she was really asking if he was alive. Of course, he was not fine at all.

The long, dark night grew darker and blacker with Nicole dozing, jerking awake, calling out to Donny, and dozing off again to repeat the process.

"Nicole, we can't go on like this! It's after midnight! God doesn't want us to be living in this fear," Donny said at last. He turned on the bedside light and picked up his Bible.

God, he silently prayed, *we need you. We need your comfort in this black hour. Show us,* he pleaded as he paged through God's precious book of promises.

"Sweetheart, listen while I read! There is comfort here in God's Word! He is always faithful!" Nicole marveled that Donny could be excited even while facing a death sentence.

"I was scanning verses in Proverbs when I found these," her husband continued. "Listen closely. 'Trust in the Lord with all thine heart; and lean not unto thine own understanding. In all thy ways acknowledge him, and he shall direct thy paths. Be not wise in thine own eyes: fear the Lord, and depart from evil. It shall be health to thy navel, and marrow to thy bones' (Proverbs 3: 5–8)."

Awe and reverence filled Donny's voice as he reread the verses. Husband and wife looked at each other in wonder and read the verses again. Neither one had remembered those promises written in God's holy Word.

"It's as if God recorded them just for us! Nicole, God is with us. Right here! Out of all the chapters of the Bible, God had me turn to this one! He wants us to claim these verses for ourselves!" Peace replaced their fear as they came to God, and the house grew still as they fell into restful slumber.

The first thing Donny and Nicole did on waking the next morning was to go to God. What a blessing to be refreshed and find comfort, strength, and peace for the unknown. They felt fortified with God's presence. Nicole began packing while they waited for a call to leave for the James Cancer Institute, a two-hour drive away.

God also sent them comfort that day through their church family, friends, and neighbors. People called. They would begin crying and say, "I don't know what to say, but we love you.

2

James Cancer Institute

January–February 2006

Donny penned the following after getting a clearer picture of his health condition.

Further tests at the hospital confirmed that I have a severe type of AML (Acute Myeloid Leukemia). For the first few days we struggled tremendously with questions. Why us? Why me?

We were also faced with a host of other things we had never considered before. Do you have a living will? Does someone else have power of attorney in case something happens to you? Do you realize that the cancer treatments may make it impossible for you to have any more children?

What? Never to have more children! Suddenly our little boy became doubly precious. Nicole and I are just starting our life together!

As we prayed together and committed our future and that of our child into the hand of God, peace prevailed. God would give us another child if He so willed.

How could we possibly handle everything being thrown at us? We quickly realized this wasn't going to be over soon. Worries flooded our minds. What would happen to our house? How would we pay our bills? Who would care for our animals? But God was in control. Miracles started happening.

On the West Coast, Michelle awoke with a heavy burden. *Pray for Donny and Nicole. Fast and pray,* God's Spirit spoke to her.

"Lord, I will," she answered willingly. "I will fast and pray as long as you want me to." After kissing her husband goodbye as he left for work, she knelt by the living room couch to intercede for Donny and Nicole.

"Lord God in heaven, you know all things. What is happening to Donny? Who is helping them? Are they facing more than they can handle? These questions are weighing heavily on my heart and mind. I come to you today, feeling the intensity of their need. Guide them, dear Lord. And give us wisdom to know how to be there for them in this very difficult situation."

Throughout the day, Michelle spent time in prayer, pleading to God to reveal His will to someone who could be there for Donny and Nicole.

"Oh, God, how will they make it? Who will support them? We are so small, Lord, and your power is so great and magnificent. Yet you say, 'Come unto me; ask and it shall be given.' Lord God, hear my prayer. I plead for Donny and Nicole . . ." Michelle continued steadfastly in intercessory prayer.

Suddenly a peace settled over her as a thought gripped

her mind. *Danny will go to support and care for them.* Michelle sat up, startled, with tears flowing and her heart rejoicing. God seemed to be speaking this message of hope clearly to her heart.

Could this be true? Would her cousin Danny really go? "Thank you, God, oh, thank you!" she cried aloud in joy and hurried to call her husband, eager to tell him of God's revelation.

When Gail returned home from work, they took their thanksgiving and joy to the Lord in prayer, asking God again to make His will clear to them. Then they called Danny.

When Danny answered his phone, he and Gail visited a little before Gail explained the purpose for his call. "Danny, my wife has been praying for hours today and wants to share something with you."

"Danny," Michelle said, coming right to the point, "I prayed for someone to go care for Donny's family, and God seemed to show me that you will." Silence filled the air while she held her breath and considered the shocking proposition she had just thrown at her cousin.

"Well, Michelle," Danny answered calmly, "I have been praying and calling out to God all day about Donny and Nicole's situation. And God seems to be telling me the same thing. I've already started packing, and I'm leaving Oregon tomorrow."

Now Michelle found herself speechlessly holding the telephone. She could not make her tongue form a reply.

Goose bumps peppered her arms. When her husband carefully removed the receiver from her outstretched hand, she threw her arms around him, overwhelmed by the manifestation of God's loving care. That night they fell asleep in the glow of having walked and talked with God.

The next evening Donny and Nicole got the unexpected call from her first cousin, Danny Wolfenbarger. "Hello cousins, guess you will be seeing me shortly." The matter-of-fact statement sounded like music to their ears.

"Danny, that's great news! When are you coming?" Donny asked.

"Let me tell you the story first," Danny answered. "When I heard you were in the hospital with leukemia, a great heaviness fell over me. Yesterday it was raining, but I needed to get away and pray for you, so I took a tarp with me and went up on the mountain into a wilderness area. I spent the day calling out to God on your behalf. As I prayed, I heard God saying, 'Go! Go take care of Donny's family. Stay until they no longer need you. Go now.' I love you, Donny and Nicole, and I've already left for Ohio."

Now it was Donny and Nicole who were peppered with goose bumps as they considered Danny's unselfish sacrifice. They marveled at how God was taking care of them!

Over the next weeks when his wife and son were sleeping, Donny opened his journal and recorded meaningful verses or bits and pieces of what was taking place.

"Fear thou not; for I am with thee: be not dismayed; for

I am thy God: I will strengthen thee; yea, I will help thee: Yea, I will uphold thee with the right hand of my righteousness" (Isaiah 41:10).

I'm beginning to accept this trial in my life. I feel more and more at peace about the situation. I am in the hands of God.

"And now I exhort you to be of good cheer: for there shall be no loss of any man's life among you, but of the ship" (Acts 27:22).

If God could preserve all those lives in the midst of a severe storm and broken ship, why couldn't He preserve my life? Oh, blessed comforting thought—He could!

Another miracle! Three people visited throughout the day, and by the time the last one left, we had received enough cash to make our next mortgage payment and pay our heating bill. It seems God is saying, "See, I have not forsaken you. I am here taking care of you. Trust me."

It is wonderful having Mom and Dad here, but I feel bad to have wrecked their Florida vacation. I know how much they look forward to spending time in their cozy trailer house in the sun.

Here at the Cancer Center, I began aggressive chemotherapy, receiving three drugs twice a day. Two weeks into the chemotherapy, the port through which they administered the chemo became infected, and I became feverish. The fever proved to be a living nightmare. For five days it yo-yoed between 103.0 and 105.8 degrees Fahrenheit.

The nurses packed me with ice, had me take cold showers,

and even tried a cooling blanket through which cold water was circulated. Nothing brought my fever down.

Then I began experiencing uncontrollable shaking known as rigors. As my fever rose, my body shook so hard the bed would shake. Terrible cramps gripped my legs. They lasted up to forty-five minutes at a time and recurred every hour or so. I was given the highest level of morphine to no avail. Nothing helped.

The nights were the worst when the hospital was quiet and patients slept. When I could not bear the agony any longer, I would wake Nicole and she would bathe me with a cold cloth, trying to cool me. I needed her touch. I don't know what I would have done without her.

Then I got worse. I had no strength left. I could barely roll from one side to the other. I could barely talk because I couldn't get my breath. My heart rate increased every day, and my chest kept getting tighter and tighter.

Will this be the last time I see my parents? I wondered as they left my room. Is this how it feels to die? My wife! My little son! I wept.

There were three days and nights during this low time when I did not sleep at all. Those nights my room turned into a whole different world. I would try to close my eyes, but when I did, I felt like I was falling into a deep black pit. I saw lights flashing and flying past me as I fell. I was in the vise of fear. I was afraid to close my eyes. I trembled. In the midst of my fear, God reminded me to lay hold on His Word, to pray, to sing. Verses like these became precious to me:

"Trust in the Lord with all thine heart; and lean not unto thine own understanding" (Proverbs 3:5).

"Thou wilt keep him in perfect peace, whose mind is stayed on thee" (Isaiah 26:3).

Our wall is literally covered with cards. "Every time I look at all these cards, I see and feel the love and prayers of our friends right here in the room with us," I told Nicole.

Once as I was reciting verses, I literally saw an image of the cross of Jesus lit up on one of the cards. *God is with me! God is right here in my room!* I reached out and grasped the mercy my God was extending to me.

During those nights when I could not sleep, I kept my eyes fastened on the glow of that cross. I would think of the words of the song: "The cross is not greater than His grace; the storm cannot hide His blessed face. I am satisfied to know, that with Jesus here below, I can conquer every foe."[1]

Clinging to these promises, I knew I could make it through the night, because I knew God would help me. With His presence I could defeat the devil's temptations. Later I told my wife, "Someone sent me a glow-in-the-dark card." Then I shared with her what I had experienced.

"You must have been hallucinating!" she remarked.

I knew she did not believe me, so I said, "Take the card, the dark card in the middle, into the bathroom. See for

---

[1] Ballington Booth, public domain.

yourself how it glows."

"Sweetheart, this card does not glow in the dark!" she said, coming out of the bathroom with incredulity stamped visibly on her face.

Then I knew. "Nicole, this is another miracle! God gave me the glow of the cross as a sign to show me I am not alone. His presence is right here in this room with me."

During this stressful time, Nicole also experienced God's intervention and presence. When they had first arrived at the hospital, she had staggered into Donny's room carrying Dallas, a packed suitcase, and a loaded diaper bag. The doctor entered behind her and abruptly informed her, "You are not allowed to stay overnight in this hospital room, especially not with a baby."

Nicole stared at him, stunned by his words. Was he really that heartless? Without thinking, Nicole burst out, "But I have to stay here! I can't leave my husband!" Tears ran unheeded down her face, and she trembled violently. Her thoughts overwhelmed her. *My husband might die! He could die any night, yet I can't be with him?*

The doctor turned on his heel and left without saying another word. Nicole and Dallas stayed. The nurses brought a mat for her to sleep on, but each week when new doctors came on duty, the same process was repeated. "You cannot stay in this hospital room overnight," the new doctor would say, but when Nicole refused to leave, the doctor would say nothing more.

Nicole found fear to be her constant companion. Would Donny die today? Tonight? How could her husband make it with his unbroken high fevers? Could he survive with his high white blood cell count and low red blood cell count? Would Donny get another life-threatening disease from all the blood transfusions he was getting? Or would the chemo take his life?

These questions continually haunted her, and she felt her whole world spinning out of control. In her helplessness, Nicole began blaming God.

Why, Lord? Why are we being punished when we love each other and have a good marriage? Lord, my husband serves you with his whole heart! Is that not enough? Why are you doing this to us? The questions hammered mercilessly, giving her no rest and taking her peace away.

Though the young mother willingly served her little family, the nights seemed to be one long nightmare. Between caring for her baby's needs and trying to bring down her husband's fevers, she got very little sleep.

Each night, Nicole gladly, lovingly, kept her husband covered with cold, wet towels in an attempt to cool his burning body. She felt terrified as she watched him shake with rigors, unable to do anything to stop the muscle cramps or the pain. She had never dreamed she would one day see her 210-pound, 6-foot-1-inch husband, who bench-pressed 300 pounds, lying in a hospital bed, emaciated, completely bald, and unable to roll over.

When her heart felt as if it was being crushed under its

load of anguish, she slipped away to a private waiting room and cried out to God. "Lord God, help us. Heal my husband," she pleaded. "I can't bear to see him suffer." She would pray the same prayer over and over again until a measure of calmness prevailed.

Though Nicole tried to hide her despondency, her sick husband perceived her struggle. Even in his weakened condition, Donny tried to encourage his wife. "Sweetheart," he reminded her, "we prayed for the past year that God would use us, and I told Him we were submitted to whatever He had for us. Pray, sweetheart," he pleaded in his exhaustion.

Nicole did pray. She tried to be as strong and accepting as her husband, but the thought of total submission was extremely frightening.

How could she submit to God's will if it meant losing her husband? *God, please don't take him! You can't! What would I do alone with a little baby?*

"This is our mission field, Nicole," Donny patiently explained when she could not find rest in their situation. "I feel God wants us to use this trial to reflect His faithfulness, to let those we come in contact with see that God is sustaining us, that He is with us, and that He cares. Won't you try to understand?" Donny pled with her again and again before Nicole grasped the magnitude of what her decision to accept the leukemia meant to her husband.

In desperation, she heeded her husband's counsel to submit to God in everything. "I do submit to you, God," she cried. "I can't do it on my own, but I do give our family into your keeping." Hope surged through Nicole as she watched Donny's tension evaporate. *Is Donny right? Is this the reason he is sick? Did God purposely place us on this hospital floor because others are facing terminal illnesses and He wanted us to reflect His presence to them?* These unanswered questions surged through her mind.

Okay, Nicole inwardly agreed. *I'm willing to share the saving love of Jesus Christ. But I hope and pray that while serving God in the hospital, Donny will be healed. What good would it do to die when he can reach so many people? God will answer our prayers for healing, won't He?*

Nicole's unanswered questions continued to torment her, but because she loved her husband, she gladly supported him in their endeavor to be lights shining in the midst of pain, trial, and possible death. When Donny marveled at God's peace filling his heart, she marveled too and felt a tentative peace.

When Donny commented, "I know I'm surrounded by the loving prayers of our church family and friends, and I'm sure it is their prayers that are giving us the strength to walk through this valley," she had to admit he was right. She found herself absorbing his faith and peace.

"We love sitting here with you!" several different nurses explained as they began stopping in for no other reason than to talk. "This is the most peaceful room on the ward! It feels so different, so special, as though there is another presence here when we enter."

"There is another presence in our room." Donny grabbed

the opportunity to witness. "Jesus Christ resides with us twenty-four hours a day, seven days a week. He is with us here, He is with us at home, and He is with us wherever we go and in whatever we face."

Donny's ready witness opened the door for many spiritual discussions, and the nurses began working on their paperwork in Donny's room just because they enjoyed being there.

"Sweetheart, can't you sense the presence of Jesus in our room with us?" Donny asked one day after a nurse had left.

"Yes, I can," Nicole answered, awed at the glow of joy gracing her husband's face.

The next entry in Donny's journal reads:

One especially bad night my face was so swollen that I could hardly open my eyes. I had severe diarrhea, and in my weakness I had to use a bedside stool. I felt painful wretchedness and inwardly cried, "I feel like an invalid! I can't walk! I can't control my bowels, and I can't even use the bathroom!" I felt tears running down my face.

"Dear Lord, I can't sleep," I prayed, "and I need my rest. Hold me, dear Lord. I hardly feel as if I can go on." I needed God's comfort. Returning to bed, I claimed it in His promises.

"Fear thou not; for I am with thee: be not dismayed; for I am thy God: I will strengthen thee; yea, I will help thee; yea, I will uphold thee . . ." (Isaiah 41:10).

"Come unto me, all ye that labor and are heavy laden,

and I will give you rest" (Matthew 11:28).

On February 3, I had another bad night. A harsh rasping sound came from my chest with each breath I took, like a file against metal. Terrified, I called for the nurses. Did I have pneumonia? Was this how I would die?

Two doctors walked in, looked at me, and then walked out without saying a word. I glanced at my wife and saw that her fear mirrored my own. A nurse returned and added more medication to my IV.

Several hours later the rattle in my chest went away, and I found I could breathe easier. My fever went down, my rigors disappeared, and I began feeling better as the extra dose of medicine in my IV took effect and my body started eliminating excess liquid. I slowly began to improve.

The day after this frightful nighttime experience, Nicole found out Donny had been given a very high-dose steroid to see if it would snap the high fever. This had been a last attempt. Donny's body could not handle much more. But God intervened, and Donny began to slowly improve. When he was strong enough to write, he penned this entry:

Doctor Jones came again to visit, bringing a bag of healthful snacks for my wife. He prayed for us before he left.

On Sunday, February 5, a chorus that my cousin Justin sings with stopped in to share their message of song. Praise the Lord! The hall simply rang with heavenly praise. Talk about uplifted spirits! I wished the half hour had gone on and on and on . . .

"Thank you, Lord, for friends! They have encouraged us in so many ways. They have helped financially. They have visited us and brought delicious home-cooked food. They've prayed with us, read the Bible with us, sent cards and letters and given Nicole breaks in caring for me. How could we live without Christian friends?

"Thank you too, Lord, for Danny. We are humbled by his sacrifice. I ask myself, would I be willing to literally move across the country and into another family's guest room to take care of their house and property? Lord, you knew how much we needed him."

And then this entry:

February 14, 2006 – Hallelujah! I get to go home!

I can't quit smiling. My smile keeps popping up, getting bigger and bigger. Home with my precious wife! Home with my sweet little boy! We will have to come back to the cancer center for more treatments later, but for now we get to go home!

"God, you have been so good to us through this time. You have cared for us! You have not forgotten us! How we love you! We will keep trusting; it is only you, God, who can keep us strong."

In researching ways to help build up my body's health, I've realized it would be beneficial to change my diet and eating habits. God started throwing information into my life, and a plan has emerged. It's been exciting to learn how we can strengthen the healing mechanisms of our bodies by consistently eating the nutritious foods God has given us. My wife and I are going to try to eat 80 percent fresh, whole foods and only 20 percent cooked foods. That means we will be doing a lot of vegetable juicing.

DADDY, ARE YOU SAD?

3

Four Weeks at Home

February–March 2006

*H*ome! What a joy-filled moment! Our family is return-ing home—together. Truly this is a miracle from God! Donny's heart could not stop praising, especially as he thought of the doctor's words. "Almost no one with your type of cancer leaves the hospital," the doctor had informed Donny in his last consultation. "Mr. Good, you are a walk-ing miracle."

Home! Donny and Nicole smiled at each other as they walked into a house decorated with hearts. Tantalizing smells wafted from the kitchen where they found a hot meal waiting in the oven.

Home? They glanced apprehensively at each other when they realized they were really on their own. No doctor or nurse was close by if an emergency arose.

Home! That night they had no interruptions—just sweet restful sleep.

Home! The next morning, inviting sunshine beckoned to them. How they had missed it! Fresh, invigorating coun-try air washed over them as they strolled around their little yard, listening to the house finches chirping their morning praises. Nicole's heart bubbled with happiness. It would be easy to trust God now. Hadn't He answered her prayers and brought Donny home?

One day Nicole ran to meet her husband as he returned from his walk. "Donny, Michelle and Gail are coming! I can't believe they're coming!" Nicole's words ran together in her excitement. "We'll get to see Caleb and Dallas together! Won't it be fun! I can't believe she is coming, with her baby due in less than three months. But they want to be with us, and this is the latest she can fly. Aren't you glad?" Nicole didn't wait for an answer but continued talking excitedly.

Yes, I am glad too, Donny thought as he smiled. His wife did need the encouragement and support of her twin's presence. It would be good to have Gail and Michelle in the community before he had to return to Columbus for his next treatments.

Five short days after Gail and Michelle arrived, Michelle went into labor and Gail rushed her to the hospital. *I wish the phone would ring! This suspense is killing me!* Nicole thought for the umpteenth time as the hours ticked by. *I'm so worried! It's already 1 a.m.!*

At 1:30 a.m. the phone rang, and Nicole shared the receiver with Donny. "We have a little girl," Gail informed them.

"How exciting!" Donny exclaimed, but before he could say more, Gail interrupted. "Our baby may not live. She was born with giant omphalacele. Her small intestines, stomach, and liver are outside her body."

The news hit Donny and Nicole like a cement block. Numbness spread through their limbs, and Donny struggled to hold onto the phone receiver.

"Michelle is okay," they heard Gail say, "but our baby is being transported to the Toledo Children's Hospital." Donny saw Nicole's eyes widen and all color drain from her face. He watched her mouth open. A wail ripped through the room when he laid down the receiver, and she crumpled into his arms.

"No! No!" came her strangled cry. "How much more is God going to do to our family? How much, Donny, how much?" All Donny could do was wrap his arms around his wife. He prayed that God would help her handle this new trial without battling bitterness.

"Let's go downstairs and waken Danny," he whispered to his wife when Dallas stirred restlessly in his crib. "He'll want to know, and I feel like we need someone to share this pain with us."

Danny put his strong hands on their shoulders as they shared the phone conversation with him. "We need to pray," he said. "We need to pray for Gail and Michelle and for ourselves." His compassion opened the floodgates of grief for Donny and Nicole. Kneeling together with Danny, they took their pain to the One who heals all sorrow and knows all things.

Several days later Donny wrote:

The morning we received the shattering phone message

from Gail, it seemed impossible to go back to sleep. So we stayed up and prayed until about 3:30 a.m. Finally, exhausted, we decided we should try to sleep, since we didn't know what the day ahead would hold.

Gail and Michelle's baby is still alive, so Tillman and Elaine Bear are traveling back and forth to a hospital again. This time it is not to visit us, but to be with their son and his family. I find myself battling the shocking situation. How can this be? This can't be possible! This can't be happening to our family again.

Gail's family moved into a Ronald McDonald house right by the hospital. We drove up to meet tiny Sadie Heather, who weighed three pounds, fourteen ounces when she was born. So tiny and so helpless! She is kept paralyzed and is hooked up to a ventilator. Her intestines are inside a sac sewn to a hole in her abdomen. But the big problem is the size of her organs. They are too large for her body since they had grown outside of her. "It will take three to four months before she will be big enough to have her organs put inside her," the doctor explained.

There we were, comforting Gail and Michelle when they had come to comfort us. I still cannot believe this is happening. "What are you trying to say to us, Lord?" My soul cries out for understanding. We are spending several days in Toledo before I need to return to the Columbus cancer center. I struggle to put my trust in God as we deal with this blow. I hardly know how to help my grieving wife.

One thought God keeps bringing to me is this—I do not

have to understand. God simply wants me to accept. By myself, I cannot accept what is happening, but as I pray for strength to accept and not question, God is faithfully answering. He has been giving me assurance of His sustaining love. He has been showing me that His ways are much higher than mine.

Nicole wanted to lash out at God. She wished she could scream. *How much does God expect me to handle? Does He want me to lose my mind?* Instead she grappled alone in the blackness of her despair.

I can't upset Donny. He would be appalled at me, she reasoned. By keeping her feelings tucked away, she felt herself being sucked further inside a huge dark hole without any way to climb out. She became bitter at God and angry and disappointed with Him for letting baby Sadie be born with life-threatening problems. *Why? Why?* She raged as she struggled for answers.

Not again! She wailed when she realized she was facing the same old problem of submission to God.

Donny grew increasingly worried and tried to reason with his wife, but Nicole refused to hear what he said. When she saw him praying, she knew he was praying for her, and it irritated her.

"Why is God wrecking our lives?" she threw at her husband, slipping further and further from His comfort.

Donny continued to pray. He pled with God, "Save my wife. Don't let the devil have her."

One day a non-Christian neighbor came to visit and

said to Nicole, "It's beyond me why good Christian people like you need to suffer! It should be happening to me, not you! Why is God letting this happen?" she persisted, waiting for an answer.

Panic hit Nicole. *What can I say? That I have been blaming God? That my relationship with God is rather strained right now?* For the first time since Sadie's birth, Nicole realized her sin. By not accepting the difficulties in her life, she had blinded herself to God's loving provisions and damaged her relationship with Him. Yet at that moment, divine promptings helped her know how to answer the neighbor in a way that would bring glory to God.

"We don't know why we have to go through painful times, but God has never let us down." Nicole was amazed at how much she found herself believing the words she was saying. "I confess that I have failed to accept what God has given us to go through, but I am realizing He has never failed me. I can testify of numerous miracles God has performed for us. For example, from the time he was born, Dallas was an extremely colicky, demanding baby. But from the first night we entered the Columbus hospital until the day we left, God touched our baby and made him more content." As Nicole continued sharing with her neighbor about the ways God had provided for them, she felt her faith being settled and strengthened. Her words rang with restored conviction as the light of God's presence graced her countenance.

"Wow! That is unbelievable. I am amazed!" her neighbor responded, her face showing her wonder as she left their home.

"Lord God, forgive me," Nicole prayed when the neighbor was gone. "I want to be willing to bear this cross, to accept your will, and to submit to my husband. I want to leave the future with you. Forgive me, Lord. Cleanse my heart from all bitterness," she prayed in contrition. Unexplainable sweet peace filled her repentant heart, replacing the inner turmoil that had been wrecking her.

Nicole hurried to find Donny and told him what had just transpired. "The joy I felt at the neighbor's positive response," she concluded, "helped me realize the source of my bitterness and doubt. The devil wants me to be discouraged. I realize now that God never forsook us, but that I walked away from Him. I'm so sorry, Donny. I have made life miserable for you."

Donny said nothing but reached out his arms to her. Together they wept tears of joy, knowing that Nicole was once again at peace with God. "I thought I was losing you, sweetheart," Donny said. "I could not bear to lose you spiritually. That pain was worse than any pain I went through in the hospital. Praise God for answered prayer! I can face anything, knowing your relationship with God is right."

Donny's next entry recorded more misfortunes.

February 23 – Danny lost his job today! And this is just one of a string of unfortunate things he's been facing. Yet Danny never seems to get discouraged!

Last week he came home with his truck's back bumper bent down and fresh scratch marks on the side. "The person behind me didn't stop in time," he shrugged.

Then on Monday he came home from work and gave me a sheepish grin as he showed me the result of another mishap. Someone had clipped the right corner of his pickup. "My fault this time," he said. "I pulled out in front of a Yukon by mistake."

And today he lost his job! Yet I'm amazed at Danny's positive attitude. "I'm trusting God," he said.

What would we do without Danny? He pays our bills. He takes care of our animals, our house, and our yard. He sings with me, prays with us and for us, and he's a great encouragement. He lifts a tremendous burden from my mind. "Thank you, Lord, for sending Danny. Bless him abundantly. He gives us his all, and he gives it joyfully. Thank you for his tremendous testimony of selfless living for you."

And then Donny penned:

Sadie looks so perfect lying there asleep. Tears fill our eyes as we watch her fighting for life. "Lord, can't you spare her? Haven't we seen enough grief?" I'm pleading for the life of my tiny niece, but I'm also praying, "Not our will but yours be done."

One day gives us hope. They think they will be able to work with her; she is doing better. The next day she is worse, and hope is gone. Up and down she yo-yos. And now we need to return to Columbus for the second round of treatments.

4

Second Round of Treatments

March 2006

Excerpts from Donny's journal:

March 13 finds me back in James Cancer Institute. Do I want to be here? No! I feel so good. But God has a reason for all this. I pray the same prayer that I've been praying, "Lord, use me for whatever purpose you choose. I am yours."

Nicole gave a little sigh as we got off the elevator at our floor. "I wish we could get our old room. Room 1032 was so nice and spacious, but I won't even expect it!"

It's good Nicole prepared herself, because we didn't get our old room but the tiny one beside it. "Guess we will just cheerfully pack ourselves into this small room," she said. Her determination is a big encouragement.

The goal of my second round of chemotherapy is to eliminate any surviving cancer cells. Then the next step should be a bone marrow transplant. Tests done during the four weeks we were at home showed I have a rare type of blood and that neither my brother's nor my sister's bone marrow matches mine. This has been devastating news. My body would have the best chance of accepting the bone marrow if I got it from a sibling. Without a transplant, I have only a 20 percent chance to live, the doctors have informed me. Satan has been attacking me with feelings of despair.

The doctors found one hundred possible matches in the National Bone Marrow Registry. This renewed my hope until I discovered how slim the chances were that my body would accept any of them. They have found one donor who would be a 9-to-10 match, but the doctors want to check out three more people to find a 10-to-10 match.

Then God granted us another miracle. A common side effect of chemotherapy is sores in the mouth. The drugs ravage the digestive system, and the patient gets sores throughout the digestive tract. The doctors said, "No one ever gets away without at least having mouth sores."

But I did. I did not have a single sore in my mouth! Were people praying? I know they were. I could feel the presence of prayers, and I know many people promised verbally to support us in prayer.

I started researching bone marrow transplants and do

not like what I found. I would receive a high dose of chemo and intense radiation to kill all the existing bone marrow in my body. They want no marrow left that is capable of reproducing. Only then would I receive the donor cells.

If, by chance, my body did accept them, they would grow and produce new blood cells. But then I discovered that no one with AML had ever survived the transplant! *Why would I even think of doing it?* I asked myself. Do the doctors feel I have such a slim chance to live without it that it doesn't matter whether I die from the transplant? Am I being used as a medical experiment?

"We need to earnestly pray for God's direction," I told Nicole.

We've prayed. We've sought God's direction, and we've asked our church family to pray with us. Once more we feel overwhelmed at the magnitude of the decision. Should I not have it done, knowing I have only a 20 percent chance to keep living without it? Or should I have it done, knowing no one with AML has ever survived the transplant?

One day I looked out the window and saw the sun beckoning. *Come outside,* it seemed to call with its cheery light. *Come outside and enjoy God's sunshine!*

Inspired, I turned to my wife and said, "Let's go take a walk, sweetheart. I can be unhooked from my IV since I'm not getting chemo today. Let's bundle Dallas up and go outside!" We acted like two excited children, but it felt wonderful to sit on a hospital park bench and feel the rays from heaven beaming down on us.

When we returned to our room, a nurse met us in the hall outside our door. "Shh! Don't panic, but you no longer have your room!" she said, and with a merry laugh she led us into room 1032!

"I can't believe it!" my wife exclaimed, hugging the nurse as we entered our old room and saw all our things arranged there. "I can't believe you moved everything for us! How lovely! We will actually be able to move around. Thank you so much!"

In this and other ways we feel the nurses' loving care for us. And it is wonderful being in our old room again! "Lord," my heart sings, "we feel your presence with us. We know we are in your care."

Friday, March 17 – We discovered a medical center in another wing we had not been to before. We found a food court there. Nicole ordered a fruit smoothie, and I got boneless almond chicken at the Chinese place. Close by was a glassed-in corner flooded with bright sunlight. Talk about a delicious supper and a wonderful spot to eat!

Danny came for the weekend, so after Dallas was in bed for the night, we went to the conference room and sang. "You two sing so well together!" Nicole cheered. "I love listening to you."

The next morning, Danny burst into our room. "Donny,

I found a great place to sing! Tell little buster here to hurry and take a nap so Daddy and I can go sing," he teased as he scooped Dallas off the floor where he was trying to escape from his mat. "The place is in the atrium," he explained. "It has high ceilings, and wow! I can't wait until we try it!"

We discovered the place was perfect, with great acoustics. Our songs soared heavenward, filling the whole area. I wondered what it will be like to sing in heaven. Five people stopped to listen to our singing and asked us to sing the song, "When Peace Like a River."[1]

"Thank you for singing. We have been blessed! Your singing was majestic!" our listeners beamed.

My own heart sang with praise, *Thank you, Lord. It feels wonderful to do something for someone else. I want to be used for your glory and cause souls to think of you.*

Words of songs mean so much more to me since my illness. Tears are often not far from the surface as the words speak to my heart, drawing my thoughts toward heaven. Singing always gives me renewed strength! In the book of Psalms, David wrote, "He hath put a new song in my mouth . . . " Praise His name! I can sing that new song of praise and trust.

The doctors and nurses tell me, "You are our most boring patient. You rarely ask for anything, you never complain,

---

[1] Horatio G. Spafford, public domain.

and your wife does almost everything for you! Do you even need us?" they teased. They do leave us pretty much alone and don't say anything about us not eating the hospital food. We are glad, because we feel better eating our homemade soups, cereals, and muffins.

"I like your setup; it looks like a little home," one nurse commented.

This hospital stay is much easier physically, but what do we do about the transplant? The decision is a tremendous burden. What if there is no match? What of the horrible side effects? Is this really what we should do? Is there any other way to fight this thing?

I think about the "code blue" alert that we hear almost every day. Code blue means someone is dying. Then I think—20 percent! I have a 20 percent life expectancy. I constantly think of the doctor's prognosis. How long until they call "code blue" for me?

March 29 – Today code blue was right across from our room. In rushed the technicians with shockers, trying to get the dying patient's heart beating again. We saw the look of horror on the patient's wife's face as she watched her husband's body rise off the bed with each shock. She peered into her husband's room from the hall. Tears were streaming down her face, but she refused to go in.

Is this how I want to die? The agonizing question kept playing in my mind long after they had removed the man's body from his room. *No!* a persistent voice within seems to say. *You do not want that done to you at the end of your life.*

It was very hard to sleep last night. My wife and I remembered the time I was close to death and what Nicole had possibly been spared.

"Lord God," we pleaded, "we are open to anything. Just show us the way."

Many times my wife and I have spent the greater part of a day singing and praying as we try to keep our spirits up. "God Hath Not Promised"[2] has become our theme song, and we sing it every day. We find ourselves clinging to Proverbs 3:5–8, the verses God showed us when I was first diagnosed.

We keep wondering why God isn't showing us what to do about the transplant. Sometimes we wonder whether He has abandoned us. But then I need to remind myself, *I cannot let Satan wage his war of discouragement against me. I dare not let him win. I have God on my side!*

After pondering God's power in this whole situation, I told Nicole, "Honey, we need to stop trying to figure out what to do about the transplant. I believe God wants us to give this whole thing totally into His hands." And that is what we did.

We are learning things about God. We're learning that when you come to the place of total submission, you need

---

[2] Annie Johnson Flint, public domain.

to be ready, because the Lord wastes no time. The very next afternoon after we had decided to stop worrying about the transplant, a total stranger telephoned me to tell me what the Lord had done for him. This is the story in his words:

"Ten years ago I, too, was diagnosed with leukemia and decided to put my life into God's hands. I went to church and my whole church prayed, asking the Lord to heal my body. I was miraculously healed and have never had leukemia since. Brother, I called because I just want you to trust in the Lord."

"How did you get my number?" I asked, intrigued.

"Oh, I've had it for three weeks. Someone told me about you, and I have been waiting on the Lord to tell me when I should call. This morning I felt the Spirit's prompting. *Call today! Today is the day.* I tried a couple times this morning, but I couldn't get you. My wife kept calling, asking, 'Did you get him yet?' I told her, 'No, but don't worry. The Lord told me to call today, and it will be today. God is never wrong.'"

I looked at my arms when I hung up the telephone. They were covered in a cold sweat. "Lord, just yesterday we gave everything into your hands, and now today I receive this phone call. I feel overwhelmed and encouraged! This is another confirmation that you care about us."

That evening Donny took his little family for a walk through the hospital. There was a place by some windows that had become special to them, and they lingered there. Donny was pondering the goodness of God when his wife reached for his hand.

"Darling, I want to tell you what was impressed on my heart today," she said with quiet conviction. "Today the Lord told me the future holds something different for us. I perceive it won't be an easy life, but I do feel God has special plans for us. I want you to know I am willing to do whatever God asks of us."

Donny felt tremendously encouraged as he listened to his wife. He and Nicole both felt unprepared for the un-known task ahead, but they were at peace as they bowed their heads. "Give us courage, Lord," Donny prayed. "You hold the future, and we give ourselves to you. Use us to bring honor and glory to you."

"How do you feel about spending the next couple of days in prayer and fasting?" Donny asked Nicole. "We know the doctors don't give me much hope. If we seek God, I am confident He will show us if I'm to have a bone mar-row transplant."

During this time of indecision, Donny and Nicole received devastating test results showing that they would not be able to have more children. "No more children! No brothers and sisters for Dallas!" Nicole wept as she held onto their precious son as if he, too, would fly away. But in the midst of this added sorrow, both of them felt God's reassurance. "Donny and Nicole, I see everything. I am in control. Put your trust in me." Peace replaced their doubts, and they had a clear answer. They would not do the bone marrow transplant.

Many people were praying that morning when Donny

met to tell his doctor he did not want a bone marrow transplant. Conflicting thoughts warred within as Donny waited for his appointment. *What should I say to my doctor when he has already said I have only a 20 percent chance to live without a transplant? He has already told me more chemo treatments are not an option. My body would only "laugh" at more. He said the only thing to do is to have a transplant.*

Donny still didn't know how to approach his doctor when he took a seat in the office, but then he heard the doctor's grave voice say, "We were unable to find a match for you, Donny." As the doctor gave what he thought was a fatal verdict, he did not know the immense relief coursing through his patient or his prayer of thanksgiving.

No match? God, you are in control! You are reaffirming our decision! Thank you, Lord, for being with us. Donny rejoiced silently. Several seconds later, however, he was shocked to hear the doctor announce, "I want you to begin six more rounds of chemo treatments, starting right away."

Chemo? Nicole sat stunned on hearing this contradictory plan for treatment.

"But doctor, you told us the last time that Donny's body would laugh at more chemo. Didn't you say more chemo would do absolutely no good?" Nicole stammered in confusion.

"Well . . . well . . ." the doctor hedged. "There may be some chance!" Looking up, Nicole found the same disbelief stamped across her husband's countenance before she heard the doctor retract his suggestion with, "Let's wait and see how things go. You do seem to be doing well, and as I said, we cannot recommend a transplant."

The Goods left the doctor's office with full assurance that God was leading them and directing their decisions. It seemed God's plan for them at this time was to forego further medical treatments and continue with their diet and lifestyle changes.

"We know this is what God has for us, for now," Donny shared with Danny upon returning to their room. "We do not know what the days ahead hold, but we are confident that God will continue to direct us as we walk in His will." Donny's next journal entry consisted of only a few short paragraphs.

March 30 – Sadie took a turn for the worse. The doctors were going to do surgery this week, but that is postponed. Our hearts bleed for Gail and Michelle, but all we can do is give words of encouragement over the phone.

I've had slight fevers the last two days. Yet I feel the Lord is truly helping me to say, "It is well with my soul whatever the circumstance." Is not the condition of my soul so much more important than that of the body?

Nicole and I talked about being bolder in our witnessing. God said in His Word, "Have not I commanded thee? Be strong and of a good courage. Be not afraid, neither be thou dismayed: for the Lord thy God is with thee whithersoever thou goest" (Joshua 1:9).

DADDY, ARE YOU SAD?

5

Why Lord, Why?

April 2006

Heavy sadness filled Donny as he wrote:

> April 3, 2006 – Sadie is in heaven.
>
> "Be merciful unto me, O God, be merciful unto me: for my soul trusteth in thee: yea, in the shadow of thy wings will I make my refuge, until these calamities be over past" (Psalms 57:1). I found this verse and thought it was so fitting for me today. We always want to ask, "Why?" Yet God says, "My thoughts are higher than your thoughts." We humans cannot see things as God does. We must trust in Him.
>
> What comfort do we get out of this? Sadie is perfect in heaven. Jesus is possibly holding her. Someday, we will all go see her.

It is far easier to write about submission to God than to live it when your heart is engulfed with throbbing pain, Donny thought as he held his grieving wife and precious son.

"I want to put my arms around Michelle!" his wife wailed. "Oh, Donny, I want to be there for them!" But

Donny was helpless to take her. Instead he held her in his arms and prayed for God's comfort.

Agony like a crushing stone settled deep in the young husband's chest. *How would Nicole handle life if I were the one who had just passed away?* He groaned under the weight of the unknown future that awaited his wife and son. *I want to see my son grow up! I want to play ball with him, teach him to ride a bicycle, go fishing with him. I want Dallas to remember going to church with Daddy . . .*

Despondency settled over him. He was startled to find himself angry with God when he had just written about God's comfort in his journal. He knew it was wrong, but right now it seemed he could not stem the flow of negative emotions. "Lord, help me! I feel totally helpless." Donny called out to God as he held his grieving wife, who could not stop crying for her sister.

God did hear. God was waiting with outstretched arms to help and comfort. As the prayer left Donny's lips, God reminded him. *Donny, I am holding you. I am holding your family, and I have my everlasting arms around Gail and Michelle.*

"Fear thou not, for I am with thee . . . I will strengthen thee . . . I will uphold thee." Quietly, reverently he quoted the precious promise and felt his anger and tenseness evaporate.

That night Donny's hand shook as he penned:

"God, my faith wavers at times. I pray, lead us."

April 4, 2006 – Nicole broke a piece off her tooth today and now has a headache. The tooth will need to be replaced. Just what we need with no income! What next?

April 5, 2006 – I want to go home! But I am having "blasts," which are abnormal cells in my white blood cell count. I am so let down. This is exactly what I had when it showed I had cancer in the beginning!

Tonight the nurse said, "Let's wait and look at tomorrow's report." She sounded positive, but I am fearful of the outcome. I was hesitant to ask what is causing it, but I finally did.

"It could be your bone marrow, or it could be the leukemia coming back," she said. My mind reels at the implications of her answer. Then God brought the thought to my mind, "Fear thou not . . . "

I know God is in control, but I still struggle with fear, knowing how easy it is for the cancer to come back. "Do you want to place yourself in human hands or in God's hands?" I ask myself. I know the answer, but fear still wants to be a part of my life.

April 6, 2006 – Praise the Lord, I'm going home! Guess what! They brought in my blood report this morning, and there were NO BLASTS! It is so exciting! We already have everything packed and are waiting for Mom and Dad to come.

Various emotions surged through me when the doctors said, "We will see you later."

Will they? Will we be back? What will we do from here? "Lead us, Lord; we can't do it without you."

Goodbye, room 1032. So long for now!

Gail and Michelle came to our house for a few days before they flew back to Oregon for Sadie's funeral. "Thank you, God, for giving us this opportunity to weep and pray together and to find strength and comfort in your blessed Word. We long to go with them, but your will be done."

6

Where the Lord Leads,
We Follow

April 2006–July 2007

"I'm staying to help. That is, if you will let me," Danny stated calmly when Donny repeated the doctor's strict orders: "No working for one year, absolutely no stress. Let your body rest and heal. You have been through tremendous trauma, and any stress could trigger the return of cancer."

Faithful Danny! Donny felt humbled as he accepted his sacrificial offer. He wrote in his journal:

> Danny picks up the pieces. He hands us his paycheck and does whatever needs to be done while I soak up the sunshine, make gallons of energizing juices, and build up stamina by taking a two- to three-mile power walk a day. It feels like I do so little while he does so much! "Lord, repay his selfless giving! Where would we be without him?"

Donny gained weight. He looked healthy and felt good. "It feels as if I have renewed energy flowing into me," he jubilantly told his wife and Danny.

"You look wonderful!" or "We would never believe you had been at death's door if we hadn't seen you there," were the most frequent comments Donny heard in the first three months. Donny was quick to reply, "I thank God each day for His mercies and for every day I am given life." Even the doctors were astonished at Donny's quick recovery when he went in for his checkups.

Then in July came the three-month biopsy report—no leukemia! Everyone rejoiced at the good news.

. . . .

"Darling! Guess what?" Nicole burst out as soon as her husband returned from his morning walk. The words spilled out before Donny had a chance to answer. "We're getting company! My parents, my grandmother, and my brother Nathan and his wife are all coming to see us. All the way from Oregon!" Her smile could barely contain her joy.

"How wonderful!" Donny answered as he gave his wife a hug. Privately, he rejoiced most of all to see his wife's happiness.

. . . .

In December 2006, eight months after leaving the hospital, Donny's checkup report came back stating that his blood levels were almost back to normal.

"Praise God! We thank the Lord for showing us what to do and for continued health improvement," Donny told friends and family members. One day Nicole heard him say, "People always say cancer is a battle, and I'm fighting for my life. But I don't appreciate the word battle. I prefer to say journey."

That statement stayed with Nicole, and she found herself thinking, *Is this it? A few months of hardship and then we are done? Can we really get off this easily? Did we just take this break from work, and soon everything will be back to normal? If this is it, why does this heaviness or foreboding stay with me?* Nicole wondered. She prayed. She felt at peace with God. She believed He was in control. But the feeling that not all was well did not leave.

Around this time, Donny and Nicole felt God nudging them to move to Oregon.

But, Lord! Donny countered. *I love Ohio! My friends are here, and my wife loves living here too. We are making payments on our house, and we love this country location.*

Insistent prompting to move continued. Together, they took their burden of indecision to the feet of Jesus. Donny was reminded that he had told God he would be willing to do whatever He asked of him. "Show us, Lord," they prayed.

The answer became clear with an unexpected phone call from a minister from Nicole's home church in Oregon. "Donny, this is Nolan Bechtel. How are things going for you?" he asked. Donny told him some about his health and the way God had been healing him. Then Nolan changed the subject in a way that gave Donny direct confirmation about the decision they were facing. "I need someone to work part-time in my office. Do you feel it is a job you could handle if we were flexible with your needs?" Nolan asked.

The invitation hummed sweetly in Donny's ear. *An office job! Lord, I didn't expect this!* Out loud he said, "We will certainly consider that, Nolan. Thank you for this offer."

Donny was excited about moving, about living where his wife would be close to her family. He was excited to be directed by God, to be doing what God wanted them to do. But Nicole felt a great turmoil inside over making the final decision, and she finally blurted out, "Donny, I have a foreboding that God is telling us to move back to where I came from because your cancer is going to return!" She could not keep her fears to herself any longer. "I know you won't make it this time! God wants us to move so I will be with my family," she cried out in trembling anguish.

"Fear thou not . . ." Donny entreated. "Sweetheart, look back at how God has taken care of us! I am overwhelmed at His care! Fear comes from Satan. God is the one who holds our future, and we need to trust Him, for I believe He will never leave us nor forsake us." Her husband spoke with assurance.

Donny's steadfast strength in God did bring comfort, but Nicole could never get away from feeling their life together would be short. She tried to give up her fear, but it always returned. Yet each time she battled with fear, Donny helped her remember that God was with them.

Then, miracle of miracles! Nicole found out that she was

expecting again! Surely this was a sign from God. Surely God would not give them this miracle baby if Donny's cancer were to return. She tried to still the persistent feeling that their time together was short.

Both Donny and Nicole were overjoyed with the new life that was coming, but for Nicole there was always a cloud hanging over their lives. She needed to give her fears to God daily or be tortured with the unanswered question burning in her mind: Would God really give them a miracle baby and then take Donny to heaven?

The end of February 2007 found Donny and Nicole packed and ready to leave for Oregon. God supplied a real need when their close friends, Jason and Lavina Smith, volunteered to transport their belongings to Oregon in their semitrailer.

When the weary travelers arrived in Oregon, Michelle threw her arms around Nicole, hugging her close, unleashing pent-up emotions in the bittersweet reunion.

"Nicole, I've longed to do this for the past year!" her sister cried, giving her another hug. "It was so hard to bury little Sadie, and then Grandmother died without you being here. But I'm thrilled we are both expecting! You with your miracle baby and me due in one month!

"And Donny! You look great!" Glad thanksgiving surged through Michelle at the positive change in his health. She thought back over the past year. She and Gail had stayed home and helped Donny regain his health by buying his needed supplements, since he could not work. It had really been a privilege, not a hardship. Now, Nicole and her family were here! It was wonderful!

Nicole did not find the adjustments of moving easy. True, she was near her childhood home in Portland, Oregon, but they had no home of their own. Everything but their bare necessities was put in storage while they moved in with Gail and Michelle. Yet tucking her struggles away, Nicole bravely tackled the work involved with running one household with two families until they could clean a small trailer parked in Gail's yard and use it for their temporary home.

March 3 arrived, and the birth date little Sadie would never celebrate became the birth date of healthy Abigail Bernice Bear. Gail and Michelle held their tiny newborn daughter in their arms, marveling in the mercy and goodness of God. New life, new hopes, and new blessings replaced the pain of a year ago when Sadie lay between life and death.

. . . .

"I've forgotten how dreary winters in Oregon are!" Nicole lamented one day to Donny as she gazed out the travel trailer window into the gray, drippy mist. "How could I have forgotten how rarely the sun shines?"

We get almost no sunshine, just cold drizzly rain day after day, week after week. Just trees, trees, trees, hemming us in, making our trailer feel even more cramped than it is, Nicole groused to herself as she faced another damp, cloudy day. *Even attending my old church is an adjustment! I need to learn to know the people all over again, and Donny is a stranger to most!*

Though she found these adjustments hard, Nicole found her hardest struggle was her ever-present battle with fear of the future. Although she had not lost her husband yet, she found herself grieving for what they had lost. They had lost a normal life. She was deprived of a husband who was able to work every day and supply for their needs. They had no home to call their own. Her dream of growing old together seemed to be slipping from her grasp. Nicole felt she could not help herself as she grieved.

It proved to be a hard winter and spring for the young mother-to-be, but her husband was always there for her. His love, his actions, and his encouragement would pull her out of her discouragement and lead her to the One who gives perfect peace. Though Donny was the one who was sick, he became a personal counselor to Nicole.

"I'm doing okay." Donny would quiet her panic when she caught him feeling extra tired or experiencing pain. As she lived each day with her husband's vibrant personality and his strong faith in God, Nicole, too, began living in the moment, asking God for help to make it through the next hour.

In July, Donny was asked to fly to Pennsylvania and give a talk at a raw food convention. He used this public speaking opportunity to also share his testimony of the miraculous touch of God in his life. Scanning the packed auditorium before him, he felt humbled to see the expectant faces waiting for him to begin. "God in heaven, touch my lips," he prayed as he began.

"What I am sharing today, I have entitled 'My God—My Miracle' because I could not have one without the other." Donny gripped the lectern on the platform where he stood before a sea of faces. It calmed him to know his parents were somewhere out there praying for him, and he knew his wife, too, was praying for him in Oregon.

"I take no credit for being here today. It is only because of God that I walked out of the hospital when the doctors said they did not know that anyone with my severe type of leukemia (AML) had ever left alive."

When Donny returned home, he was immediately asked to share his testimony and story with their new church family at Porter Mennonite Church.

"I wish you weren't giving the talk," Nicole confided as they prepared to leave for church. "It is so hard to have our feelings, struggles, and trials exposed. Especially to people we know!" she emphasized.

Donny was not aware how vulnerable his wife felt as he rose to share their story. Hearing her husband talk brought back all the memories of the hardships, pain, and Nicole's fears. She cringed to have her old friends learn of her dark times. *They will think I have no faith!* she agonized.

But as Donny continued to tell their story, she found her attitude changing. She marveled anew at God's grace and mercies toward them. Peace replaced the embarrassment. Understanding flooded her as she grasped how important it was for the church family to hear of their struggles and the miracles God had performed for them. They, too, needed to know about God's provision and presence through difficult times! The congregation sat spellbound, wiping away tears as they listened to the story of the valley Donny and Nicole had been walking through.

"I want to share something yet before I close," Donny said toward the end of his testimony. "Gail and Michelle were able to spend a few days with us after little Sadie died and before they returned to Oregon. We formed a special bond, and I believe that bond was strengthened as we spent time seeking comfort from the Word of God.

"We studied the book of Job together, and suddenly, chapter one, verse eight, became clear to me. I realized that when God asked Satan, 'Hast thou considered my servant Job?' He was saying, 'Look at Job over there. I want you to see what he is made of.'

"God allowed Satan to try Job. God wanted Job to demonstrate His sovereignty, His justice, and His goodness as an encouragement to afflicted people in all ages.

"I wondered, What was God saying about us? Was He testing us to see what we were saying about my health? Did He want to see how we responded and how Gail and Michelle responded when He took Sadie to be with Him? Were we showing an acceptance of God's sovereignty?

"Job worshipped God in the midst of all his struggles and losses. He did not wait to worship until God restored his health and physical things. What was I doing? What were we doing with our trials?

"Gail and Michelle had a favorite song that we would all

sing together. Recently it has become a favorite song for my wife and me too. I want to sing it now."

> *Day by day and with each passing moment,*
> *Strength I find to meet my trials here;*
> *Trusting in my Father's wise bestowment,*
> *I've no cause for worry or for fear.*
> *He whose heart is kind beyond all measure*
> *Gives unto each day what He deems best—*
> *Lovingly, its part of pain and pleasure,*
> *Mingling toil with peace and rest.*
>
> *Every day the Lord Himself is near me,*
> *With a special mercy for each hour;*
> *All my cares He wants to bear, to cheer me,*
> *He whose name is Counselor and Pow'r.*
> *The protection of His child and treasure*
> *Is a charge that on Himself He laid:*
> *"As your days, your strength shall be in measure,"*
> *This the pledge to me He made.*
>
> *Help me then in every tribulation,*
> *So to trust thy promises, O Lord,*
> *That I lose not faith's sweet consolation*
> *Offered me within thy holy Word.*
> *Help me, Lord, when toil and trouble meeting,*
> *E'er to take, as from a father's hand,*
> *One by one, the days, the moments fleeting,*
> *Till I reach the Promised Land.*[1]

---

[1] Carolina Sandell Berg and A. L. Skoog, public domain.

"I don't know how long God will grant me life, but I want to live each day in His will. Let's pray," Donny said as he bowed his head.

"Dear Lord, tonight we come before you recognizing your sovereignty and your justice. Lord, if someone here tonight is struggling physically or spiritually, help him to put his trust and faith in you. Help us not to take life for granted, for it is a gift from you. Lord, we are your children, and you love us. Just be with us tonight. In Jesus' name, Amen."

After the service, Marilyn Yoder, a minister's wife, said to Nicole, "Satan will not like what he heard tonight. Be prepared for his attack."

Exactly as she had foreseen, Donny and Nicole found themselves being attacked by Satan in the next few days. They both felt deep, evil powers stalking them. How thankful they were for the warning of their saintly sister, so that they could be aware of what was happening and reach out to their omnipotent Father.

After Donny had shared, Nicole found that her fear of being exposed to the church family was unfounded. Instead, the door opened wide to deeper, more meaningful friendships.

DADDY, ARE YOU SAD?

7

With Joy Comes Heartbreak

August–September 2007

Donny's heart rejoiced as he wrote:

> A home to call our own for one year! "Thank you, Lord, for this provision." We moved into a doublewide trailer owned by a single lady doing missionary work in Mexico. We moved in "amongst the stuff" and set up housekeeping. My wife is thrilled to have space to spread out before the new baby comes.

Several weeks later Donny made this entry into his personal journal.

> I'm feeling tired, and my stomach is upset.
>
> Dustin Donald Good made his entrance into the world three weeks early on September 7.
>
> A week after Dustin's birth, I lost my appetite and felt very nauseated. By the next week, I could no longer work. I felt so horrible. All I did was spend the day lying in the

recliner chair. At the same time, poor Nicole needed complete bed rest as she had a prolapsed uterus from her hard home birth. I tried to help as much as I could, but I felt totally helpless. Standing for a few minutes at a time was all I could do.

A two-week-old baby! A wife in bed and a two-year-old full of energy! "My Lord and God, are you testing me again? Are you asking, 'Will he still see my sovereignty?' "

Incredible joy had filled Nicole's heart as she held her baby and cared for him, this miracle life that had been given to them. But the next week, that joy was stripped away as she watched her husband struggle with the heart-rending symptoms of leukemia.

In place of joy, dark, black anguish overcame her. She found herself angry at little helpless Dustin for taking so much of her time when she longed to be spending it with her sick husband.

Why would God give us a new baby and a week later make my husband's leukemia come back in full force? It seemed she did not have the strength to bear this sorrow.

How will I make it without you? She inwardly screamed as her sick husband held her in his weak arms, letting her cry out her broken, bleeding heart.

Donny had continued to have regular blood tests, but although his latest results showed no blasts, other strange things showed up. A lowered red blood cell count, a higher white cell count, giant platelets, and other things told them something was not right.

"Maybe it's just a flu I have!" Donny said when they got the results from the blood work. "It can't be cancer!" But Donny's reassurances did not help Nicole. Hadn't she felt God telling her this would happen? Nicole wished she could be in denial, but the evidence was too great. Donny's skin tone was changed, and he continued to grow more ill.

Michelle, too, grew extremely worried and would call first thing in the morning and throughout the day. "Nicole, how is Donny feeling today? What is his skin color? Is he tired? Is he eating?" she would ask.

One day Donny put his foot down. "Please, sweetheart, you and Michelle have got to stop asking me how I am feeling! I know something is not right, but I don't think it's cancer! I refuse to believe it is leukemia when my blood work does not show blasts."

Doubt niggled at Donny though. He definitely did not feel well. *I'm sure this is just a result of the stress of having a baby again combined with a bad case of flu,* he told himself on good days. On his bad days, he simply would not think about how he felt. Donny wanted very badly to believe that his nightmare was over. He had just given his testimony that summer! Thoughts swirled through his mind. *Will people doubt God's goodness if my cancer returns? Lord God, I want people to be amazed at your miraculous power; I don't want a relapse that will make them doubt you!*

Since the Goods did not have a doctor in Oregon who would do the necessary blood work on an ongoing basis, a chiropractor in Portland helped them with that. When the chiropractor saw that they understood how to read their own results, he put Donny's name under his care at the lab. Donny could go in and have his blood sample taken. The lab would fax the results to the chiropractor's office. The chiropractor, in turn, would fax the results to Donny. This saved the Goods two hours of round-trip driving time each time they did blood work.

Then one day, as the routine test results came in, bad news awaited them. Blasts!

"Michelle, it's back! The leukemia is back!" Nicole could hardly talk for crying. "The blood test showed blasts! Michelle, I just want to die! Please come be with us!"

Michelle had just driven into Nolan Bechtel's driveway when Nicole called her. She and Gail had made plans to go with the Bechtels to Gail's sister's wedding reception, a three-hour drive away. Hardly knowing what she was doing, but knowing her twin needed her, Michelle jumped back into the van and drove toward Donny's house. Calling her husband, she bawled out the news as Gail listened with a sinking heart.

"Please, Michelle, drive carefully. I'll call Nolan and explain. Just drive carefully, my love. I'm concerned about *you* now."

A shroud of darkness wanted to engulf Michelle as she walked through her sister's front door and beheld Nicole's face awash in agonizing sorrow. Once more, Nicole's pain became her pain.

Why this again? Didn't you promise to heal, Lord? Did we not have enough faith? How can this be? Michelle's heart wept in anguish at the seeming unfairness.

When Gail arrived, the two couples wept together and then went to God in prayer, asking for wisdom for what to do next.

"I think you should move back in with us," Gail advised. So the next morning the sisters moved their belongings while Gail took Donny into the emergency room for a blood transfusion. Donny's blood counts were dangerously low, and something needed to be done immediately.

The doctor on call took one look at Donny's paperwork and then another look at him. "You are going to die! Do you realize you are dying?" His blunt prognosis hit Donny hard, taking his breath away.

What? No compassion? Donny thought and stammered a reply. "I know we are all going to die sometime, but only God knows the exact time." He could not believe a doctor would speak so cruelly.

The next days were hard on everyone involved. "Gail, I am as worried for Nicole as I am for Donny," Michelle cried. "Her grief is so intense she hardly eats."

"I noticed that too," Gail replied. "We need to pray, not only for restoration of Donny's health, but also that God would comfort their broken hearts."

While Gail and Michelle were praying, Donny, too, was crying out to God. "Oh, God, my God, I will not turn my back on you," he prayed repeatedly. As God reminded him of the words of Job, "Though he slay me, yet will I trust in him," Donny claimed them as his own.

Inner quietness and strength soothed Donny's turmoil as he meditated on God's promises. *My child*, he seemed to hear God calling out to him through the words of Scripture, *trust me. I will never leave thee, nor forsake thee . . . I shall be a strong tower from the enemy . . . And ye shall be witnesses unto me . . . "*

Once again the grief-stricken couple sought God's healing and asked for an anointing service. "We desire to be surrendered to God's will in our lives," Donny testified to the Porter ministers. "I do want physical healing if that is His will, but above all, I need assurance of God's clear direction."

As the service progressed, God's peace washed over the devastated couple, and they felt God touch them with spiritual healing as they surrendered their wills to Him.

After the anointing service, Donny once more went to his journal to jot down what was taking place in their lives.

We are faced with hard questions. Not wanting to make decisions on our own, we turned to the church for counsel and help.

"I know we are not members of the congregation yet, but we would like to be in the future. My wife and I need and want your advice," I told these godly men whom I trusted. I wanted their input before pursuing an option Gail and I had been researching.

"How would you feel about us going to Mexico for treatments?" I then asked. "The doctors in this country give me little hope if I take more chemotherapy treatments. They said my chances of living are 20 percent or less. The doctor who saw me in the emergency room here in Portland handed me a death sentence."

"And you would like to keep on living," one of the brothers said. "You have a young wife who depends on you. You also have two little boys who intensify your will to live. That desire is not wrong, Donny. God gives man that desire."

"Because you are a young father, I encourage you to use all the resources available in your fight with this disease," another brother replied.

Another said, "If a lack of money is hindering you, don't worry about it. I know that medical costs in Mexico are considerably less than here."

"Gail and I did check into it," I told them. "We found that the cost of an emergency room visit here is equivalent to six to eight weeks of treatments there."

"As we just said," another brother emphasized, "do not let money hinder you from going and receiving what the doctors in Mexico offer. Isn't that how the rest of you feel?" He looked over the group. Heads nodded in assent. All of them agreed.

"I personally knew others who went to Mexico when they faced what you are facing medically, Donny," said one brother. "No, God did not grant all of them physical healing, but their quality of life while they were alive still made the treatments worth taking. We will be praying for you. We will pray for complete physical healing if God so wills, but if God sees otherwise, you will experience a miracle of healing that those left on this earth have yet to look forward to," he concluded. No doubt he was thinking of his own sister's fight with cancer.

"I never use all my air miles. So many of us get miles every month from business purchases that tickets should never be a problem for you. I'm sure Gail would coordinate that," someone else suggested.

"What do you know about the treatments in Mexico?" one person asked.

"First, they give me hope of survival," I answered. "A patient has a say in the treatments that are used. Some are the same as what would be given here except they are not as rigorous. For example, I would be taking chemotherapy, but in low doses, which makes my body much more receptive. The treatment center there also stresses the use of vitamins and nutrition to build up a patient's immune system. Many different treatments are offered, but I am mainly interested in those that will build up my weakened body while I'm taking low-dose chemo to destroy the cancer.

"Maybe I have hope because I want to have hope," I admitted. "God has already enabled me to live miraculously when I was told that medically, life was not possible. I believe God can do so again if that is His will. And I have a strong inner urging to go to Mexico! I feel God wants me to serve Him there. Maybe I will not be healed in Mexico.

God only knows that, but God still has a work for me."

"Go, brother, you have our blessing. We will support your decision 100 percent." The group was unanimous.

I cannot begin to express how much this show of love and support from the church brought healing to our hearts. Not 99 percent support but 100! "And we are not even members of this congregation!" I told Nicole on the way home. "Truly, we are richly blessed."

"Thank you, Lord, for the way the church has sacrificed to take us in and provide for our needs. It is overwhelming! It is also very humbling, knowing we take so much from them. Bless them abundantly, and give us the opportunity, we pray, to help others when we can."

DADDY, ARE YOU SAD?

8

First Trip to Mexico

November 2007–January 2008

One week after counseling with the church brethren, and one week before the Thanksgiving holiday, the Goods flew to the Oasis of Hope Clinic using air-mile vouchers given to them. Nicole sighed wearily as the plane taxied for takeoff. Did she have everything they needed? She checked on Dallas in the next seat and gave another sigh, this time from relief. Laresa Good, a single church sister who was accompanying them, appeared quite capable of handling their active two-year-old.

What an added blessing to have Laresa along! Maybe the mothers at church understood my needs better than I did myself, Nicole mused as she settled ten-week-old Dustin for the flight. *Having a sister in the Lord with me does make facing the unknown a little bit easier.*

"I've never been in a foreign country, and I don't know what to expect," Nicole had admitted to Laresa when she had offered to come along and help. But Nicole could not bring herself to share the question foremost on her mind. Would the doctors in Mexico be able to help Donny, or was he going there to die? Sure, they were going to one of the most reputable hospitals with up-to-date diagnostic equipment, but would that be good enough?

Nicole pushed the haunting questions away and listened as Laresa explained to Dallas why the cars looked so tiny. *Thank you, Lord, for her gift of companionship. It means so much!* Laresa was planning to stay until Donny's parents came to visit. Then she would return home to Oregon and come back to Mexico when Donny's parents left.

A beautiful little hospital with Bible verses all over the walls welcomed and calmed the new arrivals. They also discovered that each morning the whole compound met in the chapel for prayer.

"Gail," Donny said as he chatted with his brother-in-law on the phone one day, "I'm so glad we came. Not only do we have daily prayer times, we also have Sunday morning services here. It means a lot to us to be able to spend time with God before the treatments. I know our morale has already improved.

"One drawback is that Laresa needs to stay in a motel right around the corner from the clinic. But after the boys are settled into bed for the night, I watch them while Nicole walks her to her room." *And you don't know how frightened I am!* Nicole thought as she listened to Donny's conversation. *Yes, I make sure Laresa is safe, and then I pray for my own protecting angel as I hurry back through the dark shadows alone!*

Time went quickly, and Donny and Nicole settled into

a daily routine. Soon it was time for Laresa to leave, and Wilmer and Miriam Good arrived. Dallas and Dustin reveled in their grandparents' attention, and Donny and Nicole were strengthened by their loving parental support.

After several weeks of high-dose vitamin IVs, nutritional treatments, and a blood test that showed no blasts in Donny's blood, the doctor told Donny and Nicole, "I think the leukemia is in remission again. Otherwise, how could he walk around and act as he does?"

Nicole found this hard to believe. True, the last blood test had not shown any of the blasts that usually indicated leukemia, but how could that be true when she was noticing many of the same symptoms that Donny had had the first time he had leukemia. "Please, doctor, could you have a bone marrow biopsy done?" she pleaded. "We want to be sure the blood test is correct." The doctor obliged.

While they waited for these test results, Donny and Nicole felt God leading them to the Rubio Cancer Center nearby to get another doctor's opinion.

"If you have a low percentage of blasts in your blood, I feel confident we can help you, Mr. Good," Dr. Rubio said, giving them hope.

Back at Oasis, Nicole and Donny were not shocked to learn that the bone marrow biopsy results showed the presence of leukemia. But they were shocked to find that the blood tests had not shown the presence of the leukemia when the biopsy said that ninety percent of his white blood cells were blasts! Donny was full of cancer!

Not knowing what else to do, Donny and Nicole prayed, packed their bags, and moved over to the Rubio Cancer Center.

It had been three weeks since Donny had touched his journal, but now, instead of writing in his tablet, he decided to write emails so that their family and friends could stay up to date. Here is some of what he wrote that December day:

"Dr. Rubio, you have to try to help us," I pleaded. "We have no other options. The level of blasts in my blood is 90 percent." Blasts are immature, non-effective white blood cells that do not fight infection. My body's white blood cells have gone wild. A healthy person should have zero percent blasts in the blood stream.

The doctor looked at us and at our belongings sitting on his floor, and then he said, "I can try, but we are going to have to pray."

Dr. Rubio has me on low-dose chemo. The clinics use what they call integrative medicine, a combination of treatments best suited for each individual. Since I am full of cancer, we are trying to build up my body at the same time I am taking low-dose chemo to kill the cancer cells.

So what is this clinic like? It is located across the California border in the Mexican city of Tijuana. It has rooms for ten patients. Our room is quite accommodating with a double bed along with the hospital one. There is a friendly atmosphere, and the patients learn to know each other very well. The doctors and staff are Mexican, but the doctors and at least one nurse speak English. We find the love and care they show us impressive!

The food is definitely authentically Mexican with corn, beans, rice, and chicken. The wonderful part for Nicole is all the fresh vegetables and juices available at each meal. But me? I can hardly stand to smell food.

On normal days we patients, along with our families, all eat our meals together in the dining room. If I've had a bad night with fevers or other complications, my sweet wife treats me to room service with a tray. What would I do without her dedicated service?

Rubbing shoulders daily with the other patients certainly helps a person learn to get along with people from every walk of life. It is an opportunity to get close to them, and by God's grace, I try to treat each one as a friend, though a few are so bitter at life that they are unpleasant to be around.

The highlight of the day is the evening. We have devotions with our boys and tuck them into bed. My wife and I also have a quiet time studying God's Word together, praying, talking, and even sharing tears together as we fortify ourselves for the next day.

Nicole found clinic life extremely stressful. She kept busy caring for the boys while Donny went through his scheduled treatments, which began at seven in the morning. The last one wasn't finished until eight-thirty in the evening. This left almost no time for Donny to do anything with the boys.

From twelve to three each afternoon the boys took naps, giving the parents a chance to catch naps too, as their nights were filled with complications from Donny's cancer vaccines—fevers, nausea, and other reactions. Nicole also took care of a fussy, nursing baby. "Sleep? What is sleep?" she and Donny would often ask each other.

"The big in-ground pool in the back courtyard here causes me the most stress!" Nicole explained to her sister on the phone. "Where does Dallas want to be? In the water, of course! I have to monitor him constantly as there is no other good place for him to play. I don't blame him for wanting to play in the cool water though. It gets really hot and sticky here!"

People gravitated to Donny. Usually when he was outside in the courtyard with IVs hooked up to him, other patients would surround him. Nicole marveled at his patience as he talked with them and shared his testimony.

"Talking with your husband is so good for me! I always walk away feeling inspired!" a patient told her. Others said, "We can't believe his incredible trust in God and reliance on Him! We had to tell you what he means to us."

I do know of my husband's incredible trust in God and his reliance on Him. He helps me more than I can ever help him, Nicole wanted to tell them. But she kept her thoughts to herself. Some things were too precious to share.

Other encouraging comments Nicole cherished were, "We can't talk to Donny without him talking about his God! He really makes a person think!" and, "God is definitely real to him! You can even see his faith." When life grew too overwhelming for Nicole, she drew strength from these verbal expressions, reminding herself that, despite his sickness, her husband was faithfully at work in the Lord's vineyard.

Back in Estacada, Oregon, a heavy burden weighed on Gail and Michelle when they received word that Donny was full of cancer. "Can't we go to be with them?" Michelle begged her husband. "They are so far away and with Laresa leaving soon, they will be all alone!"

That morning Gail talked to his boss, Nolan Bechtel, asking if he could have time off work to make the trip.

"Yes," Nolan readily consented. "They need you. Go to them, and God go with you, brother." In his ready answer, Gail and Michelle felt the ancient blessing that Moses gave to the children of Israel. "The Lord God bless thee and keep thee; the Lord make his face shine upon thee, and be gracious unto thee: the Lord lift up his countenance upon thee, and give thee peace" (Numbers 6:24–26).

The day they left, Gail got home from work at 4 p.m., and three hours later they backed their van out of the driveway, ready to head south. Twenty-one weary hours later, they were crossing the U.S. border into Mexico.

"Gail, this is so scary! I'll pray while you drive." Michelle gripped her armrest as her husband entered the lanes of streaming traffic. *God in heaven, keep us safe!* was her constant prayer.

Gail and Michelle had never been in Mexico before.

They were amazed that each driver seemed to have a perfect license to create his own driving rules or had the liberty to decide in a fraction of a second that it was all right to create another traffic lane in the already crowded, chaotic streets. It horrified them to find no lanes at all as they tried to make their way through the confusing maze of honking traffic and meandering pedestrians while looking for street signs they did not understand.

"Praise God! Rubio Cancer Center." Michelle let out a grateful sigh as she read the large white wording sprawled across the orange stucco front. "Gail, are you sure this is the right building? It looks so . . . so third world! Not what I visualized at all!"

But they were at the right place. They soon caught sight of Laresa, who had been watching for their arrival. Donny and Nicole had no idea they were getting visitors that day.

"I'll take you up," Laresa greeted them with a huge smile. "This surprise is going to be so much fun! Nicole is lamenting that I'm flying home this evening!"

Michelle's emotions mounted when she saw Nicole standing in the doorway of a room, looking vacantly out into the hall but clearly not noticing "who" was coming toward her. Michelle kept smiling at her sister and walking up the stairs.

"Michelle?" Nicole's eyes flew open and she blinked, afraid she was not seeing correctly. With a cry, the sisters fell into each other's arms.

Donny soon joined them, stunned at Gail and Michelle's

unexpected appearance. "You two are like angels sent from God to walk beside us," he said.

During Gail and Michelle's stay, Donny sent the following email update.

Though I experience many of the same effects I had while doing chemo in the James Cancer hospital in Ohio, I also have good days.

One highlight recently has been getting to know Wayne and Margaret Diller, whom Dallas and Caleb call Grandma and Grandpa. Wayne and Margaret's twenty-year-old daughter Frieda has lupus, a disease that is attacking her immune system. We cling together for support in this foreign culture. We have church services together. We pray and sing together, and Wayne and Margaret play for hours with the boys. We thank God for sending us parent and grandparent figures through this very difficult first time in Mexico.

Of course, the biggest highlight is having my brother-in-law and sister-in-law and their family here. Gail and Michelle plan to stay five weeks. They are like angels, literally walking with us. One day we all decided to leave the center and get a motel beside the Oasis where we knew the food was exceptional. It was a wonderful diversion to walk along the sandy beach at the U.S.-Mexico border. Huge metal poles placed almost side-by-side march across the beach and into the water, separating the two countries. Helicopters fly continually overhead, and armed boats patrol the water.

"Don't even THINK of trying to swim across! We are watching!" Their constant motoring seems to scream the message to citizens on either side. A huge wall covered with crosses and names shows the names of many who have died in their efforts to cross over illegally.

We enjoyed the day! At the end we were tired but rested.

After five weeks of treatments, Dr. Rubio came to Donny. "We have your test results back. Can you get your wife and come to my office?" Alarms started going off in Donny's head, but he dutifully followed the doctor's instructions and went to get not only Nicole but also Gail and Michelle. *If what the doctor has to say is bad news, I want them all with me,* Donny rationalized.

Who could know the emotions they individually experienced as they walked into the doctor's office? Nicole did not think she had the strength to go through the door, but God heard her silent plea for strength, and she instantly became aware of His everlasting arms upholding her.

Dr. Rubio must have detected their fears because he didn't keep them in suspense long. "We see no cancer cells, Donny," he said. "You are in remission." Their heart rates slowed to normal with the uplifting prognosis. *Thank you, God. Thank you for answering our prayers!*

Donny and Nicole did not have words to explain the hope those life-giving words brought. Only someone who had walked in their shoes could know the surge of gladness that spread into every fiber of their souls. Eight and a half weeks earlier, Donny had come to Mexico with a death notice given by a doctor at home. But now the words, "You are going to die!" had been replaced with, "We see no cancer cells."

Flying home to Oregon the morning after Gail and Michelle left was a bittersweet introduction to 2008. Donny and Nicole would need to return to Mexico for another three weeks of treatments in just two weeks. Though the doctor found no cancer cells at present, Donny would need to have ongoing treatments to keep the cancer cells from returning.

"Donny, I love our adopted church family, but it is still going to be hard to face everyone's questions," Nicole agonized. "We have been gone for so long. I hate being in the spotlight! I just want to be a normal couple going quietly about our work and attending church week after week!"

"I know, sweetheart. It is hard for me to accept the financial burden I have placed on them. We have barely lived here, yet they have given us tremendous support. I would love to take care of my own family. I would love to be able to give and help some other struggling brother instead of being on the receiving end all the time. I wonder if the people here realize what their support means to us."

. . . .

"Donny, I think your family should just stay in our home," Gail suggested on the way home from the airport. "I think your recovery may be faster if you don't need to worry about providing for your family. We want to have you with us," he encouraged.

So Donny's family stayed with Gail and Michelle during the two weeks they were home.

Fear attacked Nicole every time Donny had a slight ache or pain. A stiff neck, a stomachache—things that others would give only a passing thought—caused her intense fear.

"Sweetheart," her patient husband said as she battled these fears, "You can't let fear rule you. You have to trust in God!"

Nicole tried; she sincerely did. She longed to be free of her fears. She cried out to God for help, and He would answer, but her fears kept returning and she felt powerless to control them. When the attacks of fear hit her, she would begin trembling uncontrollably until she either vomited or had diarrhea. Through it all, Donny would patiently work through the fears with her until Nicole had regained her courage and had strength to go on.

9

Travels to Mexico

January–May 2008

After returning to Mexico, Donny opened his journal and wrote down his private struggles and thoughts.

"How will you pay the clinic bill? You have no money, no income, nothing!" The tempter mocks us in his efforts to destroy our peace. He has been throwing darts of discouragement and worry as we are once again in Mexico with no funds.

But we will not listen to him! Instead, we will bring our burden to the feet of Jesus. In doing so, we are learning that when everything is taken away, we can hold more tightly to our Saviour's hand and trust Him each step of the way. What a blessed, priceless privilege!

We have nowhere to go but to God. And as we take our needs to Him, He has never once let us down. Every time a bill needed to be paid, the money was there to pay it. Every time my wife's burden seemed more than she could handle, God sent someone to lift it. God's presence, His grace, and His mercy manifest themselves daily.

January was almost over when my parents called. "We

have enough air miles to cover tickets for your family. Do you think you can come to Florida between this treatment and the next?" they asked.

"Let's go!" Nicole said eagerly. "I've been dreading the thought of returning to the dark trailer in Oregon," she confided.

"Warm sunshine sounds more inviting than the rainy Oregon winter," I agreed, so as soon as the three weeks of treatments were finished, we left for Florida from the San Diego airport.

What healing God gave us during that time! Our bleeding hearts and weary bodies received a reprieve from the battle we were fighting. We rested, we enjoyed each other and our boys, and we formed a closer bond with my parents.

Even in Florida, Donny and Nicole found others with cancer, and Donny did what he did best. He shared his testimony and helped others understand what he had learned about the body's ability to heal itself.

When Nicole's cousin Danny joined them in Florida, the two men took up their mission of singing for the sick.

Lord, do we have to leave? Nicole's heart cried as their time to leave drew close. *I want to keep this bit of paradise a little longer!* Her husband's health improvements were incredible. She wanted to stop time. Her heart yearned to preserve this happiness, never to return to the unknown future and the suffering and pain that she feared was awaiting them.

Donny and Nicole were scheduled to be back in Mexico in three weeks, but neither of them could bring themselves to leave Florida. So they extended their stay for an extra week before boarding the plane for San Diego.

. . . .

One cultural difference Donny and Nicole found frustrating in Mexico was how often an answer like, "Just a minute" or "today" ended up meaning "tomorrow" or later. Promises concerning time just didn't seem to mean the same thing there as they did in the United States.

One especially trying day, Donny emailed a little poem to Gail.

My Dilemma

Here I sit all brokenhearted,
Waiting to get my consult started.
Scheduled once, he showed up late;
Scheduled twice, said was a "mistake."
I scheduled thrice and met the doc.
But then he said, "I can't; I feel too shot."
I was feeling, *Me oh my!*
But thought I'd give it one more try!
I called to see for sure this time,
If the appointment would be mine.
Oh, yes! The time is still today,
But doc has had a long delay.

Donny and Nicole once more faced the decision of whether they should stop the chemo treatments. They were weary of the side effects. In their indecision, they called out to God in prayer and asked their family and friends to pray that God would give them clear direction. In the end, they decided to discontinue them.

"At least we will know if I can get along without them," Donny said soberly as they left the clinic for Oregon.

. . . .

"Who works at the clinic in Mexico? What is the staff like?" were two frequent questions the Goods heard from friends and family members at home. Donny and Nicole enjoyed giving others a glimpse into their lives by telling about the clinic workers.

"Well, there's Sandea," Donny said, happy to introduce his favorite nurse. "She knows almost no English. She spends countless hours in the tiny nurses' station trying to get a vein or cleaning out my port bandage. I teach her some English words, and she in turn teaches me Spanish ones.

"When we returned to Mexico from Florida, Sandea broke into rapid Spanish and hugged our whole family! I declare Dustin simply grows faster because of all the hugs he receives from her.

"Then there's Dr. Rubio. A person is instantly attracted to him with his sparkling eyes and calm, positive outlook. He offers so much hope you just can't stay down! Though

Dr. Rubio acknowledges God, he does not claim to know Jesus. Nicole and I miss the spiritual connection we had with the doctors while we were at Oasis."

"Then there is Dr. Rubio, Jr. He is much more serious than his father and is about Donny's age," Nicole said, taking up the narrative. "Both doctors will often say, 'Donny, you are our best patient!' and I've seen them pat my husband on the back as they say this."

A month later Donny was filled with deep sadness as he typed.

We had not been at home for even three weeks when we both knew all my symptoms were back. I saw Nicole slip into the deep, dark hole of grief.

"How many times more can I handle this?" I asked God. "Isn't two recurrences enough? Will we be able to get it in remission again? Lord God, our little boys!" Having Daddy sick all the time is very hard on Dallas.

We both cried and pled to God for direction. "Do I resume chemo, Lord? Show us your will!" Calmness replaced my agitation as I sought God. His love overwhelmed me, and I felt God saying, "Donny, you are not finished yet. I still have work for you to do in Mexico."

Ticket vouchers were given to us, and we were once again flying south. As soon as Dr. Rubio started chemo, Nicole saw the blanket of leukemia lifting off. When leukemia suppresses the body, it feels somewhat like a bad case of flu smothering the whole body. I have no energy, and it takes extreme effort simply to move.

The "lifting off" can be felt and seen as my body responds to treatment. When the suppression dissipates, energy begins to flow and my body relaxes, releasing me from what feels like a tightly wrapped cocoon.

The doctors are still hopeful, and hearing them fills me with hope. Every time we find ourselves in a difficult situation, God brings people into our lives to help keep up our courage.

I must write about Juan Carlos. In addition to the doctors, he is one of the people who keeps our spirits up. Juan Carlos is the driver who picks us up and takes us back to the airport each time we fly. He has become a caring friend. He is also the groundskeeper at the clinic, so our boys follow him around. Dallas asks him many questions, but Juan patiently answers each one.

Juan also plays a big role in helping me recover. Every time I return for a set of treatments I require two or three platelet transfusions. Juan willingly goes into a room where he undergoes the two-hour procedure needed to separate his platelets from his blood. He comes walking out of the room with a big grin on his face, carrying his bag of platelets, which he hands to the nurse.

This is a huge blessing because by receiving a single donor's platelets, my body is less likely to reject them. Would I be as willing to do the same for someone I barely know?

One hot, sticky morning Nicole took both boys upstairs

to Donny's room at the clinic so she could put Dustin down for a nap. "Dallas, stay right here with Mommy," Nicole firmly told him as she jiggled her fussy, tired infant. "You can't go anywhere until I put Dustin to sleep."

Oh, for a rocking chair! she thought wearily as her baby refused to settle down. Humming often helped him relax, so she jiggled and hummed without noticing that Dallas quietly left her side. A bit later she did notice him though, when he came crowding up close to her, wanting to touch her. When Nicole looked down at him, she saw that his little face was white as a sheet.

Now what? she wondered. *What mischief has he done?* But Dustin was just settling. She needed to finish with him before tending to Dallas. It seemed whenever she was tending Dustin, Dallas sensed extra freedom!

Gently she laid sleeping Dustin down in his portable crib. Looking around their room, she saw no sign of anything wrong, so she took Dallas's hand and they went downstairs to be with Donny in the courtyard where he was getting his IV.

"Mrs. Good, you are one fortunate lady!" Olga the nurse called out when Nicole entered the courtyard. "God must be watching out for the son of my favorite patient!" She shook her head before enveloping Dallas in another hug.

Nicole smiled at the nurse whose care and love for them radiated like sunshine. "Did something happen?" she asked. "Did Dallas do something?" Her little son stood like a statue, staring up at her out of worried blue eyes.

"Dallas, what did you do? Tell Mommy. Tell Mommy now!" she exclaimed in alarm. But Dallas's eyes only grew bigger and rounder.

"I think he too frightened to talk." Olga patted Dallas's head. "But I'll tell you. God surely watched out for this one! I came out just as the worker who's fixing the roof catches him! Your son, falling, falling, from concrete ledge under your room window! But roof worker is walking below. God is watching this one!"

Nicole's eyes grew as wide as her son's. A shiver of fear raced through her as she looked up two stories to the narrow foot ledge running along the entire length of the building. She looked down to the cement where she was standing.

"See?" Olga pointed to where their window was indeed standing slightly open. "He fell from up there!"

Nicole scooped her son into her arms, trembling at what might have been, but praising God for the roof worker.

"I must thank the man." Her voice shook with emotion. Turning to Olga, she found herself enveloped in another of her famous hugs. "It is true, Olga, God is watching out for us, each one of us. I am so thankful!" Nicole told her.

10

Learning to Rejoice

June 2008

"Nicole," Donny said, "I feel so good that I'm going to skip having another painful biopsy. I really don't believe I need to have it done to prove that the cancer is gone. I already feel like I am cancer-free!"

They had just heard Dr. Rubio declare, "I am confident you are again in remission," and with those words they joyfully prepared to leave Mexico.

Their joy was short-lived, however.

This can't be happening already! We have hardly been home! Donny's mind was in turmoil. *One good week! And here we are in the plane again, heading south!* He reached for his wife's hand, intertwining their fingers. His heart bled for her and the boys, but exhaustion overpowered him, and he was too tired to talk.

Instead he decided to write a letter:

Dear family and friends,
Leaning my head back against the plane seat, I close my eyes and let my thoughts drift back to the events of the last week.

On Friday the sun shone, and I felt exhilaration as I mowed our lawn. When had I last been able to do a man's job? *Please, God, this is what I long to do!* my heart sang. *Thank you for giving another time of remission.* The hum of the mower sounded like music as it throbbed beneath my hands.

"I'll help you fix your fireplace," I readily offered Gail when the lawn lay smooth and trim. He has done so much for us, and I jumped at the chance to help him.

Saturday I woke up feeling very tired after my hard day of work, and Sunday I felt even worse. Every day after that I found myself going downhill.

"Can't you at least call Dr. Rubio?" my wife implored, afraid of the signs I showed and remembering the skipped biopsy. For her sake I did make the call.

"It is too quick for the leukemia to come back, but to be safe, we could at least do a bone marrow biopsy and see," my doctor suggested without a trace of urgency.

"We think you should go," Gail encouraged me, "but let me talk to Nolan first." As soon as Gail replaced the receiver, he said, "Yes, you need to go. Nolan offered his Southwest vouchers. God is definitely pointing toward going. Let's get your tickets."

Things happened fast. It was 11 a.m., and our flight left at 4 p.m. We had two hours to get ready and leave. Mom and Dad Smallfoot and Gail and Michelle came to our trailer to help us pack. By 1:30 p.m. we were ready.

"I think we are getting this down to a science!" I

attempted to joke, but my sweet wife could not see anything humorous in the situation.

My thoughts fly heavenward as our plane reaches altitude and levels out. I reflect on this verse from the Psalms, reminding myself it is for every situation. I will close with it. "This is the day which the Lord hath made; we will rejoice and be glad in it."

"The doctor says my leukemia is back," Donny told Nicole reluctantly. He hated giving her the news. "He feels I overworked myself when my blood counts were still low. This gave the cancer a chance to grow, but he is confident I will get back into remission."

"Sweetheart, I do not understand this." A chill came over Nicole. "Each time the leukemia returns, you lose ground and never regain your health to the point you had reached in your January remission." Numbness began closing in on her, and she tried to push away the stark reality of what she was saying.

Sunday afternoon Donny wrote:

Sunday, June 22 – How do you rejoice when you are in a clinic with no one else of like faith? How do you remain in good spirits when you know your family and friends are at home singing and worshiping together, and your heart longs to be with them?

Today it is a struggle to accept where we are, to accept our situation and what lies ahead, but this verse from the Psalms keeps coming to my mind: "This is the day which the Lord hath made; we will rejoice and be glad in it."

"Lord, four days ago I needed to remember to rejoice. Today I need to remember even more. With your help I'm going to do it!"

Monday, June 23 – I sit in a clinic looking forward to a week of treatments. Not too appealing . . . but God didn't promise an easy life, did He? I try to keep this concept in mind as I look at my situation. Our salvation cost God His Son. So what I endure is little in comparison.

"Daddy, are you sad?" Dallas stands in front of me as I sit with an IV running in each arm, knowing I have to endure this for twenty-four hours for the next seven days.

"Yes," I answer as I watch my poor wife trying to get things ready for bed while Dustin sits on the floor crying. I'm overwhelmed at not being able to help her. My son begins to pull off my shoes and socks. He brings me his blanket and teddy bear. He crawls up on my lap and puts his hand in mine.

"Does your head hurt, Daddy?"

"No," I answer.

"Does your shoulder hurt?" he asks next.

"No," I answer again.

"Do your eyes hurt?" This time I hear confusion in his voice. He is wondering where else Daddy could be hurting.

"No, son, my heart hurts," I tell him. He sits quietly, making no comment until Mommy comes out of the bathroom.

"I am making Daddy feel better," he informs her, then silently keeps holding my hand while I long to take my precious innocent son into strong arms without scars and needles.

"Daddy, I am going to read you a story," he says. He climbs down and returns with one of his books, his sweet voice telling me his favorite story—his attempt to make my hurts better. I sit listening, trying to stem the heart-broken helplessness tearing my insides apart.

"Oh, God, my God, must my boys never have a normal daddy?"

The Goods prayed each day for the new family in Room 1 who seemed to be lonely and hurting. They learned that the husband and wife were named Roberto and Rosa. The couple had two children, a five-year-old boy and a four-year-old girl. Roberto was very ill and had come to Mexico for treatment after exhausting all help available in the U.S.

"No one seems to talk to Rosa, so I do," Nicole shared with Donny as they ate dinner together. "She seems very fearful and lonely. I'm thankful, though, that our children and theirs play well together."

Donny and Nicole also learned to know the couple in Room 2. Simon arrived at the clinic in a coma. He had cirrhosis of the liver due to excessive alcohol consumption. Since arriving, he had started vomiting blood.

"What is ahead for him?" Donny wondered aloud. "Nicole, we must share God's comforting promise of eternal peace and everlasting life. I don't think he has long to live."

As Donny and Nicole befriended their close neighbors who suffered both physical and mental agonies, they found their spirits battling for them. "This is why God placed us here," Donny said with confidence after returning from singing and praying for a patient named Jerry, who was battling a tumor. Several days later, Jerry's wife Kathy excitedly accosted Donny with the good news.

"Jerry's tumor is shrinking, and the feeling in his legs is returning!" she beamed.

"Praise the Lord," Donny rejoiced. Alone with Nicole, he prayed, "Lord, keep your healing hand on Jerry. We pray that if it is your will, Jerry would experience complete healing. Above all we pray that he would know what it is to be healed spiritually."

The Lord also gave them Estella to love, but she did not seem to want any love. She was a heavy smoker who was going through withdrawal. Since she was not allowed to smoke in her room or the courtyard, Estella would walk around like a caged animal, saying accusing, untrue things in a loud voice.

One day Estella got a glass of water before going outside to smoke. Just before leaving the compound, she purposely dropped it on the cement, sending shattered glass everywhere.

"Her nerves are fried," Delia, the clinic's cook, remarked grimly to Donny and Nicole as they eyed the mess left for someone else to clean up.

"But how are my beautiful babies?" She turned to Dallas and Dustin, who eagerly accepted her attention. Delia loved receiving kisses from the children, and they loved giving them to her.

. . . .

One morning Donny found himself in the throes of discouragement. *Didn't I tell my wife I felt God had a work for me to do here? How can my outlook change so quickly? Why does the devil always attack when I want to be a light for the Lord? Oh, Lord, don't forsake me!* became Donny's fervent plea as he sought God's help. God answered, and the discouragement abated.

Several days later Donny was alone, once more struggling with discouragement that seemed bent on taking away his peace. He turned to his computer and typed this email to his friends:

June 26, 2008 – Simon's wife came crying to us today. She is very sad as her husband continues to fight for his life and lies in bed hollering.

"Simon is having mental problems," she confided through her tears. "The doctor says when the liver is bad it releases things into the blood that go to the brain."

My heart bleeds for these people who are a part of our lives. My own life feels in turmoil. I want to be a witness as opportunities come, but how can I be when I, too, feel empty and discouraged?

After sending the email, Donny opened his journal and bared his soul.

"Lord, I need you! It is hard to raise a family in this situation. My wife and I seem to be losing our closeness. All I can do is sit here, doing nothing! She is so busy with the children. I am frustrated!"

As I wallow deep in the mire of self-pity, I think of my friend Jason. Healthy and doing a job he loves, he is supporting his family. We grew up together, went to school together, even worked together. Why me? Why do I have to be singled out to suffer like this?

As Donny finished writing the last sentence, he felt ashamed. Did he really think he knew better than God what was best for him? Donny bowed his head and poured out his heart to God.

Some time later he returned to his unfinished entry and wrote.

Darkness of soul threatened to engulf me when God in His great mercy reached down to me, a mortal unworthy of His continued mercies, and reminded me of the promise: "Commit thy way unto the Lord; trust also in him; and he shall bring it to pass" (Psalm 37:5).

Suddenly I was ashamed of my complaining spirit. How could I have forgotten my promise to God? I told the Lord I was willing to do whatever He asked of me, but because I wasn't happy with how things were progressing, I ended up pitying myself.

Humbled, I bowed my head, seeking forgiveness. "Lord God, you are my God! I want to bring glory to your name here at Rubio's Cancer Center. Give me a heart to love and understand the hurting people we have contact with. Give me opportunities to share your salvation message with lost, seeking souls . . ."

I rejoiced as the light of God's presence surrounded me. I began singing:

> *Be not dismayed whate'er betide,*
> *God will take care of you;*
> *Beneath his wings of love abide,*
> *God will take care of you.*
> *Through every day, o'er all the way;*
> *He will take care of you . . .* [1]

Feeling uplifted and encouraged, Donny longed for his wife and boys to return from their walk. He couldn't wait to tell Nicole how much he loved her and appreciated her care and support.

"Daddy!" Dallas burst into the courtyard. "Mommy bought you a popsicle!"

Thank you, Lord. I am so unworthy! And Donny reached

---

[1] Civilla D. Martin, public domain.

out to receive the gift.

Later that afternoon as Nicole walked down the hall, she found Rosa standing in the hall outside her room. When she stopped to talk to her, Rosa began crying.

"I don't understand why! I don't understand why my Roberto is not healed!"

Sadness welled up in Nicole. She wished she could take away her neighbor's pain, but she could not.

"Rosa, I want to be your friend," she offered. "I don't understand why either, but I do know that God is with us through all our heartaches. He loves us even more than we love our husbands." She put her arms around Rosa, not knowing how else to comfort her.

That evening after the boys were sleeping, Donny shared with Nicole the things he had been struggling with and the victory he had received. "I feel able to pray and witness again!" he told her. "I've determined by God's help to faithfully do both. As soon as I'm finished with these twenty-four-hour IVs, I want to spend more time singing with the people here. It seems the hymns touch them first. After listening to God's message in songs, they feel free to share their struggles and are more open to me reading from the Bible and praying for them. Honey, today I felt God telling me clearly, 'Donny, this is your mission!' "

Nicole smiled as she watched her husband's face light up with excitement. Tucking the sleeping boys into bed, they opened their Bibles for strength and fortification before beginning their renewed mission among their neighbors.

Donny and Nicole Good (right) on their wedding day, with Gail and Michelle Bear (left) and Danny Wolfenbarger (center).

Donny Good's smile was contagious.

Donny takes a moment to cherish son Dallas.

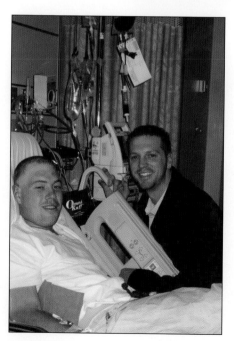

Dr. Jones visiting Donny at the James Cancer Institute in Columbus, Ohio.

The Goods leaving the James Cancer Institute.
Nicole's cousin Danny unselfishly helped them
whenever he was needed.

Dr. Antonio (Tony) Jimenez at the
Hope4Cancer Institute in Tijuana, Mexico,
was touched by Donny's faith in God.

Donny with Dr. Rubio and Dr. Rubio Jr. at the
Rubio Cancer Center in Mexico.

Donny developed a friendship with platelet donor,
Juan Carlos, who was the Goods' taxi driver and the
groundskeeper at the Rubio Cancer Center.

Donny and Danny brightened many lives by singing
and testifying of Jesus' grace.

Dustin,
a miracle
baby, is
admired by
his father
and brother
Dallas.

Donny, Nicole, and boys with Donny's parents,
Wilmer and Miriam Good.

Floyd and Dee Smallfoot enjoy their grandchildren,
Dallas and Dustin.

Nicole's twin sister Michelle and her husband Gail poured
out their love and support to the Goods.

Donny's brother Jerry and his family encouraged the
Goods with a visit to Mexico over Donny's birthday.

Delbert and Melissa Derstine, also in Mexico
for treatments for Melissa, became close
friends with Donny and Nicole.

The Goods' last family photo,
taken on the Oregon coast.

"Donny, could we visit a little with Roberto and Rosa?" Nicole asked. "She said he is very, very low."

"I have a heavy burden for Roberto's soul," Donny shared as they walked down the hall with his trailing IV stand. "But sweetheart, I feel free as a bird! Almost!" He laughed quietly and clasped Nicole's hand tighter. "As soon as I am unhooked from this tube, beware! I plan to enjoy my freedom to the max!"

When they arrived at Roberto's door, they knocked and went inside to chat. Donny soon turned the conversation to spiritual things. "Do you have Jesus in your heart?" Donny plainly asked Roberto.

"Yes," Roberto answered in a weak, whispery voice.

"Are you afraid to die?" Donny probed further.

"Not for me. But for my wife and children," he answered again as he looked at his weeping wife sitting beside him. Conversation was limited, but the couple seemed happy to have Donny quote Bible promises of the Christian's assurance of heaven.

"Can we pray together before we leave?" Donny asked. Both husband and wife nodded gratefully, and they seemed in better spirits when they told Donny and Nicole good night.

In the following days, Donny wrote these short entries in his journal.

June 28, 2008 – Jerry and Kathy were discharged. "Lord, bless Jerry with continued health as they return home."

113

June 30 – Dr. Rubio told both Roberto and Simon they are stable for now, but we all wonder how long their lives will last. Simon's wife has seen so much sorrow. Today Nicole put her arm around her and said, "We are praying for you and your husband." She didn't answer, only went away crying. Simon continues to holler, and it is hard on the rest of us to hear him.

July 1 – Another month! If you add together all the weeks we have been in Mexico for treatments, it comes to a total of ten months. Will it ever end? We have spent Thanksgiving, Christmas, New Year's Day, Valentine's Day, and Nicole's birthday in Mexico.

Simon has been released. They are going back to the States as his end is near. *When will my time be?* This question often comes to mind.

"Come," Rosa beckoned to Donny four days after their evening visit with Roberto. "The doctors took out all of Roberto's IVs. We are going back to the States."

Donny and Nicole were shocked at the change in Roberto. His labored breathing filled the room as Roberto lay staring into space. His hands were curled in a fetal position. Not knowing what else to do, Donny took one of Roberto's hands into his. Roberto gave a light squeeze, letting him know he was thankful to have him beside him. When Donny tried to take his hand away, Roberto held on, so Donny sat beside his friend and prayed for him and the family.

"Let me take your children so you can pack," Nicole suggested. Rosa agreed and began packing. She struggled to do the work though, so Donny ended up helping her.

Late that afternoon the paramedics arrived, but as they started to move Roberto, he suddenly stopped breathing. It was all over. Rosa stood in the hall and wailed, "My babies, my babies, what will they do without a papa?"

"Papa, Papa. We want Papa!" the children sobbed.

In spite of the anguish and sorrow filling the hall, there was a sense of God's overshadowing peace. No "code blue" screamed over the loud speakers. No technicians raced into the room with shockers in a frantic effort to restore life. Instead, the hospital staff offered sympathy, their tears mingling with those of the bereaved family.

"What do I tell my children?" Rosa asked Donny.

"Tell them their papa is with Jesus," he encouraged. "Roberto said he had Jesus in his heart, and when I sat by his bedside, he calmly held my hand," he reassured her.

Rosa seemed relieved by these words of encouragement. "Can you come into the room with us while my children say goodbye to their papa?" she asked.

Lord! Donny's heart cried out for help. *I can't do this! I have never looked at a dead body! It has always been a dreaded fear of mine!* His flesh recoiled at the thought. He hated attending funerals. Only once in his lifetime had he attended a viewing. It had been his grandmother's, and his parents required him to go. But though he had been at the viewing, he had never once gone near the open casket.

But this request was different. He knew they could not desert Rosa. Grasping his wife's arm, Donny walked to the bedside where Roberto's body lay. As Donny looked down at the body, he found it was not something to dread. He felt a sense of peace, and he knew God was walking beside them in this hour of trial. *Is Roberto now looking into the face of his Jesus?* The thought filled Donny with awe.

Nicole wrapped her arms around Rosa as the women wept together. When they left to return to their room, Donny and Nicole took Rosa's children with them to save them the trauma of seeing their father being taken away.

As they made their way back to their room, Donny noticed that Roberto's brother was sitting in the hall with his head in his hands. Silent tears rolled down his grief-stricken face.

Donny stopped and sat down on the floor beside him. "Roberto became my friend, and I learned to love him too," he began. The man looked at him receptively and Donny continued. He began by sharing about Roberto's readiness to meet Jesus. This seemed to be a new concept for the sorrowing man. He seemed to know nothing of salvation, but he listened eagerly, nodding his head in understanding as Donny explained that Jesus was waiting with open arms to forgive and accept every person who comes to Him.

Roberto's brother seemed glad to have Donny pray with him. After he had prayed audibly, Donny said another prayer in his heart. *Lord, I have sown your seed of truth. I pray this seed will grow. I do not even know Roberto's brother's name, but you do. Help him remember the truth he has just heard, and may he seek you with a hungry heart.*

It was 11 p.m. when Donny and Nicole finally got to bed. Both of them were physically and emotionally drained. As he drifted to sleep, Donny's last thoughts were about his wife. *How will she deal with this death tomorrow?* He was well aware that her fear of death and dying hindered her acceptance of his illness.

But he need not have worried. "Donny, I have such a peace this morning," Nicole told him early the next day. "Seeing how God was with Rosa yesterday took away my fear and filled me with peace."

Nicole's words sent a thrill through Donny, and he couldn't help but notice that her shining eyes reflected her inner transformation. "Well, Nicole, I need to confess to you that I, too, have always had a fear of death and dying," Donny shared. "Last night was the first time I stood beside a dead body. I felt that God was with me, and after last night my feelings on death are different. There is a sense of peace replacing the dread."

With hands entwined, Donny and Nicole praised God for this small victory. Soon afterward, they sent this letter of victory:

Nicole and I believe we know the "why" of our returning to Mexico so soon in June. God wanted us to be here for Roberto and Rosa. Going through the valley of death with them has changed us. Both my wife and I feel at peace and accepting of my AML. It is one thing to say you're accepting it; it is another to feel it with the heart, which I believe we are doing now.

Are our struggles completely over? Does this mean no more discouragement or fears? I don't think so. This is not heaven. Satan will tempt us. He wants us to lose faith. God created man with the drive and will to live, to fight for life until the last breath is drawn. So we need to fight the fight of faith as long as there is breath and seek the Lord's strength and help to be faithful. I have a mission yet to accomplish for God.

I will give you an update on Jerry and Kathy. I know you have been praying for them too. Kathy called us today with the shocking news that Jerry is in critical condition. Flying home caused him to get a blood clot in his leg. He started with a fever on Sunday and is experiencing severe chest pains. He has a bad infection in his blood, and he is in an induced coma.

How rapidly things can change! Satan threatened to return our fears with a vengeance. "This is what will happen to you!" he mocked.

We can never think we have it together. We must take each hour, each minute, and leave them in the hand of God . . .

In his personal journal, Donny wrote:

Blessed, encouraging news! Tremendous encouragement!

From one single phone call. My heart is singing. I am praising God! I hung up the phone with unspeakable joy and a great load lifted from me. Only God knew my discouragement about my finances and the debt I was incurring through the treatments. And now this call, this overwhelming answer to my prayer!

"Hello, Donny, this is Lavern Miller," the caller said. "I'm calling you about a men's meeting last night. I wanted to let you know that all the brethren here at the Porter church are very supportive of your continued treatments. We all want you to keep on doing what the doctors recommend. Be assured, we as a church believe God will supply the needed funds."

I just sat and held my phone. Does Lavern have any idea what his message means to us? Does the Porter church know? They are definitely fulfilling God's command: "Bear ye one another's burdens, and so fulfill the law of Christ."

"Lord God, reward these dear brethren for their sacrifices. I am not worthy of such love. And my boss, Lord. I have hardly worked for him at all, and yet he gives us a check each month as if I were working full-time. Lord, their care for us is great. We have never had to pay for a plane ticket! Every need has been met! Bless them, and use my life, Lord, to glorify you, that the sacrifice they are making will not be in vain."

One day Donny and Nicole went to Revolution Street, the tourist area of downtown Tijuana, Mexico. What a diverse place! It was filled with all kinds of restaurants and shops. Tired, but refreshed by the change of scenery and diet, they returned to Rubio's.

"Can you do something to cheer up 'Grandma'? It is her eighty-third birthday, and she is so sad to be in the hospital," a nurse whispered to them the minute they entered the clinic.

"Why, yes! We will stop at her room and cheer her up!" Donny was quick to offer. Before Nicole could protest, she found herself at the lady's bedside helping Donny sing "Joyful, Joyful, We Adore Thee." Like a wilted flower opening, the elderly lady's eyes brightened and her sadness evaporated as she drank in the words. Shyly reaching out her fingers, she caressed Dallas's hand resting on her armchair. By the time they ended with, "We wish you a blessed birthday and many, many more," her face was wreathed in smiles. Nicole gave her a hug, and Donny patted her arm saying, "God loves you very much. Don't ever forget that."

Later that same evening, the lady's granddaughter came and begged, "Please come and sing again. Some of our family brought Grandmother cake and ice cream. She says to tell you your songs cheered her up very much, and she wants you to sing for her family now!" Donny and Nicole felt a little shy about attending the party with strangers, but again they went and ministered in song.

. . . .

Why does it seem like every time I win a victory, I am plunged into the depths of discouragement? Donny asked himself as he opened his journal and vented his personal frustrations.

It would be easier to NOT be human! We long to go home, but the doctors want me to stay. My platelets are still pretty low. Gail and Michelle would like to come, but they hardly have the money. He even talked to Nolan and the ministers. They, too, felt someone should be with us for my next round of chemo. Groan! I feel so upset!

I'm upset because my being here is a hardship on Gail and Michelle. I am upset because people have to share their time and their money. I am simply irritated and upset at life!

That evening he opened the journal again to add:

"Thank you, Lord, for my wife!" We had a long talk. As we cried together and prayed together, I realized my irritation was a way of asking, "Why? Why do I have to be sick? Why do I have to cause other people, our family, our church, so many problems?"

Then Donny sent another public update.

I never introduced Dr. Smith before, so I will now. Other patients do not like her very well. "She doesn't budge an inch!" is their general consensus. We have found the opposite to be true, however. She is our day doctor, and she loves our boys!

Each time we come back to the clinic she beams a welcome. "Your being here is a highlight for the entire center!" she exclaimed one time. She often sneaks us fresh, warm, made-from-scratch flour tortillas. We have learned to love her too, and maybe that is why she bends over backward to make things easier and cheaper for us.

Now, I will tell you about my catheter miracle.

My veins have almost given out because of all the chemo treatments. Typically when a catheter is put in, it is left in for only two or three days. But the last catheter we put in has been in for over a week! I have been receiving blood, platelets, and chelation during this time, but still no pain or redness. Only God could do it.

"This is totally unbelievable!" the nurses and doctors said.

I happily informed them, "It is a miracle from God."

Even in these circumstances God is able to show Himself faithful.

11

The Love of Friends

"**M**ommy, I want to go home. I want to be with Caleb and Sassafras." Dallas's wistful pleading wrung Nicole's heart. She knew he missed his cousin and their dog. How could she cheer him up when she wanted to go home too?

They were sitting on the stairs waiting for Gail's family to arrive. Dallas rested his chin in a cupped hand, a frown plastering his usually sunny face. Nicole could not give him the answers he wanted to hear.

"Mommy! Caleb's here!" Instant happiness erased his prior gloom as he dashed to meet his cousin. *Oh, to be childlike!* Nicole longed for a life of such simplicity.

It was late afternoon the following day. Nicole was sitting by Donny's bedside whispering, "Lord, thank you." Tears of relief slipped unheeded down her face as she watched her husband's color returning and saw that his nausea was subsiding.

Her thoughts returned to her wish for childlikeness the previous day. *If only it were possible to forget your problems in an instant!* But Nicole could not wipe out the terrifying memories of the last few hours. They had decided to celebrate Gail and Michelle's arrival by eating supper at the Sirloin Stockade, an American-Mexican buffet restaurant with a fair-sized salad bar. It had been a wonderful change of menu, but something in the food had not agreed with Donny, and he had had a rough night.

In the morning, Donny had woken up with fevers and chills, and by late afternoon the doctor prescribed a blood transfusion. Then things had really gotten bad.

If only they would not have insisted on trying to use a large catheter! I know they said it would help the blood pass quickly, but it was horrible! Nicole shivered at the memory. The nurse had tried and tried to find a vein in Donny's arm but couldn't. She then probed for a vein in his leg, but the catheter would not go in. Finally, they returned to the arm and succeeded, but the only way the catheter would stay in was if the nurse held it.

By that time Nicole had not been able to bear seeing her husband suffer any more excruciating pain. Beads of sweat had peppered his forehead. He had sat in exhaustion, his eyes closed, too weak and nauseated to move. "Please," she had begged, "can't we just let him go upstairs and lie down? I will hold the line for him if that will help."

"Thank you, God," she had whispered when the medical staff had agreed. They had let Donny lie down in bed with the life-renewing blood flowing steadily. Now as she watched her husband continuing to improve, she repeated, "Thank you, God."

By evening, Donny felt fine, and the two couples looked at pictures of Gail and Michelle's wedding that they had brought along.

Have we changed that much? Donny wondered to himself. *It's rather sad to see how happy and carefree we were then, but I guess that is just life. What is God trying to teach us?* He pondered the unspoken question before pursuing another line of thought.

Most other young-married couples we know have not experienced any real sorrow or problems. They get married, have children, work, and go to church.

Why, Lord, do I keep battling with discouragement? Every day I am having these struggles. Little things seem like big things. I get on top of my feelings, but then, before I know it, I am struggling with the same things again! I pray, Lord, not my will, but yours, be done.

Donny's thoughts turned to the sacrifice his brother-in-law had made to come. Gail and Michelle had planned on spending their anniversary at the coast, but after talking to Donny and Nicole, they had cut the anniversary trip short and come to Mexico to be with them. They were so unselfish!

Unknown to Donny or Nicole, the real reason Gail and Michelle had given up their vacation was their realization that Donny was battling depression. "Not Donny!" Michelle had told her husband. "I can't believe it! He never shows anything but a positive outlook!"

"I know," Gail reflected. "I have never known him to

stay discouraged." But Gail and Michelle were barely at the clinic when they realized that Donny was indeed battling with depression.

Is Donny giving up? they wondered as they prayed and tried to be supportive. Then the doctors told them that the drugs Donny was taking were affecting his emotions and causing the depression. Gail and Michelle stayed for two weeks, both of them glad they had come to the clinic instead of finishing their vacation at the coast.

One day while Gail and Michelle were visiting, the two couples experienced what they later named, "The Great Catastrophe."

Gail and Donny were in the dining room, working at their computers, when Donny happened to glance up at the mirror above them. When he did, he saw two little boys, Dallas and Caleb, reach up and grab hold of the side railing on the buffet table behind Donny.

"Michelle!" he yelled, and watched, transfixed in horror, as the boys simultaneously lifted both their feet to swing. The empty table rose off its two back legs and started tipping forward. Michelle whirled around when Donny yelled, but it was too late to stop the horrendous crash of breaking glass as the glass canopies used to shield the food trays hit the hard flooring.

"Help! Help!" Nicole screamed as she raced to find two scared little boys looking up at her amidst broken glass. Blood ran down Dallas's face where his lip was split open, but Caleb looked fine.

"What is wrong? Are they hurt? The poor dears!" Five staff members came running into the dining room talking at once. As soon as they saw that no one was seriously hurt, and that only the canopies were shattered, they relaxed and helped the boys escape from their pinned position.

"Let me put a stitch in Dallas's lip," the doctor said when it refused to quit bleeding.

"I'm sure it will be all right without stitches," Donny assured him, feeling his son had experienced enough drama without enduring a needle. "Thank you, though, for offering. I think the best thing we can do is put these boys down for a nap!" Dallas's crying stopped, and a nurse brought a soothing piece of aloe vera plant to hold on the cut.

Nicole had instantly turned a ghastly white and almost fainted on seeing all the blood. "I can't even carry Dallas upstairs," she lamented as she took a seat to regain her equilibrium. "And the broken canopies! I'm so sorry!" Nicole apologized.

Delia, the cook, and the clinic's handyman, Keiko, dismissed her words with a wave of their hands. "No problem, it doesn't matter. What's important is that the boys are fine."

After Gail and Michelle had returned to Oregon, Donny sent out the following updates by email.

Has this round of chemo killed a lot more leukemia cells? I wonder. I'm feeling stronger with energy returning. I'm able to handle these treatments with little nausea. Dare I hope the worst is past? God is good!

My veins are so shot from all the treatments it is hard to find one. We think we are out of options when another good vein pops up. God is good!

Nicole had a filling fall out. She went to Dr. Hernandez, a dentist, and he also fixed another cavity. He dismissed us with, "No charge!" God is good!

We have learned to appreciate the new arrivals. Sam and Janelle Hostetler are here because she is receiving treatments. It is wonderful to have fellow Christians to share with. God is good!

Friday, July 23, 2008 – My brother Jerry and his wife Melrose and their two children arrived today! Dr. Rubio is letting me wait until Monday for an active vaccine because I usually get a reaction, and he knew I wanted to enjoy the weekend with my brother.

Jerry's family and we invited Sam and his wife to join us for supper at the Seafood Mexican Restaurant. The band was so horrendously loud we could not hear each other talk, so we just enjoyed the wonderful food.

July 26, 2008 – My red-letter day! I turned twenty-eight today! Here is a brief review of the past week.

On Sunday we had a service of Bible reading and singing downstairs because one of the patients requested it. "That was a tremendous encouragement! Thank you!" Bill and Dawn said afterward, giving us hugs.

On Monday afternoon we had what I dubbed "Our Beach Dilemma."

Jerry, Melrose, Nicole, and I decided that going to

Rosarito Beach would be a great way to spend the afternoon. We were excited. Neither Nicole nor I had ever been there.

"Yes, yes, I show," our taxi driver assured Jerry in broken English when we asked if he could show us where we needed to get off. So when the taxi stopped somewhere in town, we looked at each other, wondering. "Beach?" This was definitely not the beach!

"I stop here. You get off. Beach just down road," the taxi driver pointed. We exited the taxi and began walking. We walked and walked and walked and then walked some more!

"Beach just down road," Jerry mimicked. "Now we know—just down road is equivalent to a good mile or more." By this time we needed supper, and there was nothing to do but walk the long way back to the main road.

"Ahh! Food!" I inhaled the aroma of the steaming beef burrito on my plate.

"Ugh! That tastes rotten!" Nicole sputtered, spitting out her bite of guacamole. "I had better test your burrito, Donny," she said as she cut off a piece. "Oh, no, that tastes off too!" To be safe we ended up eating just beans and rice.

By now it was 8 p.m. and high time to get back to our rooms. Going outside, we waited for a taxi, but each driver said, "We are full," and then left without any passengers. We found out later that we were on the wrong side of the street to catch a taxi going the direction we wanted to go.

"What is going on?" we asked each other. Finally we crossed the road and discovered we needed to go downtown first in order to get a taxi home. It was now 9 p.m.

"I will never go to Rosarito Beach again! You won't drag me there!" my wife vowed.

A taxi! *Thank you, Lord!* We got in. "Can you please drop us off on the other side of the bridge?" I asked when the driver stopped on the opposite end of the bridge from where we needed to be.

"No. Not possible! I stop here. You walk across bridge to other side." I checked my watch, and it was 10 p.m. All I could think of were tomorrow's headlines—"Americans Attacked While Crossing Bridge!"

"Never be out at night on foot. It is not safe." Those instructions had been drilled into us since the first time we stepped foot in Mexico. The night was frightening. Here we were, four adult Americans with four little children on a deserted bridge in a foreign city. We were alone, but not alone, because our God was with us.

We prayed as we walked across the dimly lit bridge. We prayed as we waited for a taxi, and we rejoiced with thanksgiving when we found a taxi willing to take us home. "Thank you, God. You are so good!"

Jerry and Melrose left now, and we feel a big hole. We have promised each other to keep in touch. I'll never forget one conversation we had as my big brother offered the sympathy my heart needed. Breaking into tears, he said, "We had no idea what you were going through! We are so sorry!"

12

Challenges

August–November 2008

Returning to the clinic for his ongoing treatments gave Donny the needed incentive to continue what he called his "journey" letters.

August 20, 2008 – Yes, we are back in Mexico for my seventh set of treatments. The past three weeks at home were not nearly long enough! We were not able to attend church or see anyone because I did not feel good and because people in the area had chicken pox.

September 1 – I have not been able to write with my hands tied up in IVs.

October 12 – Another red-letter day—our anniversary! Mom and Dad Good came on October 4 for two weeks. With the hospital being fairly empty, they stayed in Room 7.

"Not many men take their wives to Mexico to a resort for their anniversary!" I quipped today as I handed my wife six red roses. "One rose for each year!" I felt pleased with myself for seeing the roses on our way home from the Sirloin Stockade, where my parents had taken us in honor of our anniversary.

The roses were not the only thing that made Nicole feel treasured that day. Donny also composed a song that he sang to her.

"Now it is my turn!" she laughed as she handed him a card she had made. "Darling," she said, "I love the way you made this day extra special, but I find that every day you are here with us as a daddy and a husband is special to me." Love shone from her eyes.

That Sunday, the staff allowed Nicole and her mother-in-law, Miriam, to use the kitchen to make an anniversary meal. What fun the two women had as they cooked for just themselves in a furnished kitchen.

"How are you really doing, Nicole?" her mother-in-law asked as they waited for the meal to be ready.

"I find it hard to be staying in the same room we did when we first came for treatments," Nicole admitted. "It wants to bring back the hopeless feelings and struggles we had then."

"I'm sure," Miriam sympathized. "I never thought of that."

"Also, I try to keep a strict schedule, but it is hard when I am always the one who needs to take charge," she confided.

"But Nicole, you are doing so good!" her mother-in-law said. Though her words were a healing balm, Nicole wondered if Miriam had any idea how much she had depended on Donny to keep up with the daily routine in the past.

"You know I'm not a take-charge person," she admitted. "But having a strict schedule does help me keep on top of things."

The weeks slipped rapidly by until Wilmer and Miriam left for their Ohio home. Donny and Nicole returned to Oregon briefly and then were back in Mexico before Donny sent out another update to their friends.

Dear friends,

Here we are again. Home and back down to Mexico. Sadness fills us. Two more patients passed away since we were last here.

We had a meeting with the ministers at Porter before we returned. They wondered how things are going for us. We have so little involvement with the church and feel terribly alone when we need to work through personal issues. My wife and I are working hard on submission-leadership roles within the home.

We appreciate the church's love and concern for our physical and spiritual welfare. Unconditional love is only made perfect through our commitment to Jesus Christ. I believe we can master every situation with God's help. "God is our refuge and strength, a very present help in trouble" (Psalm 46:1).

Roberta Zito has been the only other resident here beside our family. Last Sunday my family had a service in Room 10, by the fish tank. We listened to a message on CD and sang hymns of praise. That evening the nurse came and informed us, "Roberta's not doing well. She is returning to the States."

My poor wife was in the hall as the ambulance attendants

wheeled her out. Roberta looked terrible, moaning and groaning in pain. Nicole came into our room completely traumatized. Tears and emotions that she tries to stuff down boiled over.

"Donny, I've seen so many people die!" She was crying, and I was thinking, *Is this how it will happen with me?*

That night we gathered comfort from the devotional book that takes us through the Psalms. David experienced much fear. David knew what it was to feel deserted by God. When we finished reading, we were inspired to keep our eyes on God.

The very next day we received word that a dear brother in Christ, Enos Zimmerman from Missouri, finished his earthly journey. He left behind five young children. Our hearts cry out, "God in heaven, give the family comfort, wisdom, and guidance."

We also cry for ourselves. "We are open to your leading, Lord. Give us your wisdom and guidance as well. "

God knew our need for companionship and sent our bishop and his wife, Edwin and June Bontrager, to comfort and strengthen us for four inspiring days.

Dallas immediately warmed up to them. He loved having them read him books and playing with "new" toys June brought along. He even called them Grandpa and Grandma. On the last day of their visit, it seemed Dallas sensed they were leaving because he became naughty and extremely emotional.

One day in November, Donny felt extremely helpless. He wrote of his trials in his personal journal.

"Lord, I need patience with my son. I feel so badly for him. This upheaval of family life affects him emotionally. Lord, at times like these I have a hard time accepting the disruption of our family life. Why do our poor children have to suffer as well? Are we giving them enough stability? Will they learn to love you? Do our sons feel security from us? How can they, Lord, when we ourselves struggle with the questions and the fears?"

"Daddy, I want to go home! Why can't we go home now?" Dallas cried and cried after Edwin and June left. I feel so sorry for him. Our routine is forever broken, and he needs a stability I can't give him. Heartbroken at what I can't fix for my boy, I plead with God, "Lord, don't let this instability have a lasting effect on our sons. Help me be a good father and give our sons security in an insecure world."

DADDY, ARE YOU SAD?

13

A New Year: 2009

January–July 2009

Greetings to our dear family and friends!

Thank you from the bottom of our hearts for your prayer support, your letters, and your love gifts. Where would we be without them?

This is my first visit to Mexico in 2009. How do I feel starting out the New Year by visiting a cancer clinic? Well, my negative human side says, "It is terrible! Horrible! Why can't I be normal? Why does my life have to consist of round after round of suffering? Why do I have to battle to stay alive when others so nonchalantly live their lives?"

Then my positive Christian side says, "Look, things could be worse! I could very well NOT be here. I could very well NOT have a loving, supporting church body, family, and friends who support 110 percent.

"Where would I be without the people who pay for the supplements and treatments I take? Where would I be if I didn't have God? When I think of all we do have, I feel VERY blessed!"

A clinic friend, Carolyn, said to me, "Donny, there are

other people who do not have cancer who have it a lot worse than we do!" That spoke to my heart. When I think about my cancer, I begin to feel sorry for myself. Feeling sorry for myself makes me feel angry, impatient, and rotten. Rather, I need to focus on being glad that I am alive!

We have met our new resident "neighbors," fellow Christians! Though no one from Oregon could come down with us, the Lord provided middle-aged Christian people to be here. Getting to know Carolyn and Mark is already a highlight. The last time we were down we were the only overnight patients. It does get lonely when we are here alone!

February 9 found Donny and Nicole in Florida with his parents. Donny spent a great part of each summery day drinking up the sunshine. Even though his energy level did not bounce back like it had the previous year, Nicole remained hopeful, especially after seeing Donny's blood tests.

The first blood work Donny got done in Florida that winter shocked the doctor. "If you had not told me your history, I would have said you have the blood of an athlete!" The doctor could not believe the results, so he did another test to see if the two would match. When both tests gave the same result, Donny said to the doctor, "It is God who has put His healing hand on me like this."

Five weeks seemed to fly by, and once again the little family boarded the plane for San Diego.

Thank you, Lord, for the healing time in Florida. Thank

you for putting a song within our hearts. Donny closed his eyes, letting the words of song drift through his mind.

> *I care not today what tomorrow may bring,*
> *If shadow or sunshine or rain;*
> *The Lord I know ruleth o'er everything,*
> *And all of my worry is vain.*

Refrain:
> *Living by faith, in Jesus above,*
> *Trusting, confiding in His great love;*
> *From all harm safe in His sheltering arm,*
> *I'm living by faith, and feel no alarm.*[1]

In May, Donny sent out this email:

What do you do at a Mexican clinic on Mother's Day? I wanted to do something special for my wife, so I helped the boys make a "flower bouquet" out of paper. I traced around the boys' hands on paper with a highlighter. Then we cut out the shapes, which were our flowers! The stems were folded paper colored green. The "vase" was another piece of paper folded and taped, all held together with medical tape.

It was fun for the boys to do, and Mommy's eyes were rather teary when we presented our gift. I did remember to bring a card from Florida!

Tillman and Elaine Bear are coming from Ohio for four

---

[1] James Wells, public domain.

days. What a tremendous boost to our emotional wellness that will be! God is always ready to give us what we need at the very time we need it.

"Of course you can't come to Mexico without visiting a fabric store, Elaine! I'll take you," Nicole bravely offered when Elaine asked if the shops were close by.

Oh, no, do I really know how to get there? Nicole quickly hushed her own doubts with positive thinking. *Well, I have gone numerous other times,* she told herself. *Besides, we will take a taxi, and the driver will know the city!*

"I think I had better go with you women," Tillman gallantly proposed as they made arrangements to leave.

"We will love having you along to carry our fabric!" Nicole quickly answered, leaving Tillman wondering what he was getting himself into.

"Do you know any Spanish?" Nicole asked Elaine after trying to converse with the taxi driver. "I don't think our driver knows any English."

"No." Elaine's eyebrows lifted. "I really don't."

"This might prove to be an interesting shopping trip!" Nicole laughed.

Leaving the clinic and finding the first store was no problem, because Nicole knew where to direct their driver. Then, before leaving that store, Nicole had the English-speaking clerk write the address of the second fabric store on a paper. Off their taxi driver went, pulling up in front of a little store which did not sell fabric!

"No, no." Nicole used the one Spanish word she knew he would understand. Pointing to the paper, he just shook his head, indicating that he did not know where the store was. She heard him talking rapidly to a radio dispatcher before he handed the receiver to her. A voice speaking English sounded in Nicole's ear. She gladly gave the address, and off they went again, but soon their driver was looking uncertain.

"We are in trouble!" Nicole informed her passengers as they stopped along the road without any fabric stores in sight. "I have no idea where we are!"

Amazingly, the driver in the stopped car behind them spoke English, and he knew where the store was! Finally, after they had traveled a long time and seen a lot of the city, their taxi delivered them to a fabric store.

"Have you seen enough fabric or should we try to find another store?" Nicole asked Elaine as they waited in line to have their purchases cut.

"I've browsed enough," Elaine answered. "And knowing Tillman, I'm sure he will agree!"

The next day Donny innocently inquired, "Tillman, would you and Elaine like any more city tours?"

"I think we have seen enough of Mexico!" Tillman declined.

Grandpa and Grandma Bear, as the Goods called them, got in on one more bit of excitement before they left for home. One day Nicole left the dining room with two tired boys in tow. "Time to take afternoon naps!" she sang.

Dallas jumped into bed to cuddle with his blanket while Nicole reached for a diaper to change Dustin.

Suddenly, there was a loud thud! Dallas's piercing scream sent Nicole whirling around to see her son hanging over the edge of the bed with blood gushing out of his mouth. Weakness immediately hit her. She kept telling herself, *Don't faint! You can't faint!* Over the years, fainting had been her normal reaction to the sight of lots of blood. *Stop! You have to get help! You dare not faint!* she sternly commanded herself.

"Dallas, stay here, I'm going to get Daddy," she warned above his sobs. Nicole raced downstairs. Taking a deep breath to still her pounding heart, she walked into the dining room and whispered in Donny's ear, "Come this minute; don't wait a second." Without waiting for Donny to reply, she left the dining room and raced back upstairs to Dallas's hysterical cries.

Donny jumped up from the table in a panic. *Something is definitely wrong!* Without thinking what he was doing, he went tearing out of the dining room, IV tubes trailing him. Halfway up the stairs he heard his son's screams. His body automatically kicked into second gear, a gear he did not know he had. Off flew his sandals as he tore the rest of the way to their room.

Bursting in, he saw blood all over his son, the floor, and the side of the bed. By this time the whole compound knew something had happened, and as Donny stuck his head into the hall to yell for a nurse, she was already running toward them with a roll of gauze in her hand.

Nicole's hysterical explanation would have been comical to her audience if Dallas had not been filling the background with heartbreaking sobs.

"I can't find it! I can't find the tooth! I don't know what happened! My back was turned . . . I heard a bang . . . he's missing his tooth . . . I think he swallowed it!" Nicole's words spilled out like rapid-fire bullets while she searched on her hands and knees for the missing tooth.

Donny picked up Dallas, telling him calmly, "Everything will be all right," while the nurse gently cleaned up the blood.

Just as the doctor arrived to help, Nicole triumphantly held up the missing tooth. "Here it is!"

"It looks like part of the tooth stayed in," the doctor said upon examining Dallas's mouth. "You'd better take him to the dentist."

"Mommy, I wanted to get my teddy on the stand!" Dallas blurted between his sobs. "I leaned over the rail and smacked my mouth hard!"

"I see what happened, son," Donny assured him as he examined the railing. "The rail was not latched correctly, and when you leaned on it, it gave way. Ouch! Your tooth even chipped off a corner of the nightstand!"

An hour later the Goods left the dentist's office with their son beaming in delight at the plastic mouse he carried in his hand. "Your broken tooth is inside this mouse. It is yours to keep," the dentist had explained when he gave the excited little boy his treasure.

Dallas proudly carried the mouse everywhere. He showed its contents to everyone he met, whether they were friends or perfect strangers!

On May 19 Donny sent out another letter.

My veins are no good. We just faced a tough decision, but my wife and I cried and prayed to our God, and we decided to go ahead and have a port put in. I will explain. The port is a catheter that is put under my collarbone into a big artery that drains into the heart. Having one presents the risk of infection, but we must leave it in God's hands.

They will draw blood from the port, so it is a relief to be free from pokes and sticks. The doctor says it will take at least three months until the scar tissue in my veins heal.

Lyle and Carolyn, a couple from home, came today. We barely know them, but it shows us the love of the church at Porter. They chose to come and spend their anniversary trip with us! Wow! I hope they realize the tremendous blessing their sacrifice is to us. "Bless Lyle and Carolyn abundantly, Lord. Bless them in the way they have blessed us."

Although Dallas and Dustin were usually carefree and upbeat, Donny's ongoing illness definitely took a toll on them as well. Sometimes Dallas seemed sad for no apparent reason. "Daddy, make me a doggy out of balloons," Dallas sniffled one evening. His forlorn voice was full of sadness. No smiles. No sparkly eyes of mischief. He looked lost and lonely, not at all like a carefree three-year-old who lived with two loving parents. Donny wanted to weep with Dallas when he asked again, "Can you make hotdogs too? I want to feed them."

When Nicole told Michelle about Dallas's sadness, Michelle summed up how Dallas must be feeling.

"Life is far from normal for him," she sympathized. "When you are in Mexico, Donny is busy with doctor appointments and treatments. When you come home from Mexico, Donny is recovering from the treatments and has no energy to play with him. And you have to spend most of your time taking care of Donny.

"I wonder what he thinks when you are here in Oregon and he and Dustin come over to our house. Uncle Gail plays with them and their cousins, while his daddy lies on the couch or floor doing nothing. What is he thinking when Donny can't sit and eat at the table with the rest of us?"

Weeping washed over the telephone lines as Nicole listened and realized all the negative implications her husband's illness was possibly having on their precious sons. She thought about the ways they were trying to cope and wondered, *Should we be doing things differently? But what would we change?* She hung up the receiver, but her mind kept returning to the rough times when the two families spent most of their days together. Sometimes they had simply moved in with Gail's family, living with them for several weeks. Other times, when they were at the trailer,

Michelle would stay with them through the day hours, and Gail would join them after work in the evenings. If Donny had had a really bad day, Gail's family would end up staying for the night.

While Nicole contemplated the relationship their family had with her sister's family, Michelle was doing the same in Oregon. She kept thinking about her sister as she pondered their circumstances.

Does Nicole understand how much her husband has touched our lives? Michelle wondered. *It's as if our lives are all intertwined as one. Nicole, Gail, and I are all desperately helping to keep Donny comfortable as he fights for his life.*

Michelle thought of the times she had tried to encourage her sister by telling Nicole what Donny meant to them. "We don't find it a hardship to be helping; rather, we often think of Donny as an angel in our lives," she had told her sister.

Not many times did they hear Donny complain or question God. The strength and determination he had to be a positive witness for Jesus to his family were certainly an inspiration and challenge to them and to others. She recalled one of the recent conversations that had taken place the last time Donny and Nicole were in Oregon.

"Gail, I'm worried about you! You are doing so much for us! Are you getting enough rest?" Donny asked. It broke their hearts to hear his concern in the midst of his own suffering.

Another evening Donny had shared, "My prayer is that

the valley God is allowing me to walk through will never cause my family to be bitter. I want them to see God's presence with us, for God is indeed here."

Michelle thought of her brother-in-law's battle. Donny had more than his illness to deal with. She knew he spent hours in loving counsel with his wife, helping her find peace and courage to go on. She knew that Nicole, by her own admission, often found it hard to trust God completely. Donny's steadfastness was a beautiful example not only to Nicole but to Gail and Michelle as well.

Her thoughts veered to the times Donny felt well enough to join them in Bible reading and prayer. Invariably, the men ended up in a Bible study or all four of them would sing together. Those were precious times of sharing and even crying together.

Yet, in spite of Donny's steadfast faith, Michelle saw how his illness had a disturbing impact on the boys. It affected Dallas especially, and her mother heart prayed for her little nephew who had to be so brave.

. . . .

Several weeks had passed since Nicole's phone conversation with Michelle. Donny and Nicole and their family were home in Oregon again visiting Nicole's parents. Donny looked out the picture window and noticed the rain had stopped.

"Come quickly!" he called to Dallas, who was putting a puzzle together at the dining room table. "The storm is over, and there is a rainbow in the sky." Father and son walked outdoors to find a beautiful rainbow stretched across the horizon.

"Do you know what the rainbow means?" Donny questioned his son.

"What, Daddy?" His little boy looked up with wide-eyed, innocent wonder.

"This rainbow is like one God showed Noah after the Flood. Remember when God promised Noah He would not destroy the whole world again with a flood of water?"

"You mean God won't ever let anyone die?" Dallas asked.

"No, son." Donny's heart broke a little at the implication of his son's question. "People may still die, but the rainbow means God will never forget you and me. God still loves and cares for us no matter what happens."

"Oh!" Dallas replied, satisfied with his father's answer. He ran back to finish his puzzle.

And what does it mean to me? Donny mused as he gazed at the fading colors. *One thing is sure. It always takes a storm to see a rainbow.*

During their time in Oregon, the Goods sent out the following email to concerned family and friends.

Doctor Rubio extended our home stay to six weeks! "Thank you, Lord!" And our next visit to Mexico will be only eleven days long! Many of you may not know, but for the last while we were returning to Mexico every three weeks and staying at the clinic for two and a half weeks.

Lately our time at home has been increasing to four weeks at home, two weeks at the clinic.

WOW! It feels as if we are starting to see the light at the end of the tunnel.

I have not returned to work yet and probably won't for at least the rest of this year and part of next.

It is amazing how God continuously cares for us and blesses us. He never lets us go hungry or cold. We also know that the treatments and all that we do would not be possible without the love and financial support from you, our family and friends. For that we say a huge THANK YOU. May God bless each of you!

I do have a prayer request for you. Please pray that God would protect me from catching any virus or sickness while my blood counts are down. Pray, too, for Nicole, that God would give her strength and courage. This time period is always hard on her as she sees me go through the side effects of the treatments. Each time after treatments, my body goes through fevers and gastritis. Also inflammation takes up residence in any little sore, etc.

I will share with you an answered prayer, or what I call one of God's miracles. Normally at the beginning of the fourth week after I finish treatments, I feel what I call "The Jump." This is when the bone marrow really kicks in and the counts begin to go up. I wake up in the morning feeling more energetic and motivated to get things done. This time I was starting into week five and still had no jump. All my inflammation had disappeared, but I had little energy and felt very, very tired.

I was unable to go to sleep, and in our concern we talked to Gail and Michelle, sharing our worries. That night after talking to them, I went to bed and fell right to sleep for the first time in weeks. The next morning I woke with a song on my lips.

I HAD FELT "THE JUMP!"

The amazing power of prayer! We found out Gail and Michelle had spent a long time praying for us that very night. Who but God, our great God, hears and answers the prayers of His children?

On Father's Day, Donny opened an envelope with a smile and read:

> *Donny Good, Estacada, OR*
> *Happy Father's Day*

My Dearest Love,

Happy Father's Day, Darling. God has blessed me so much in giving you to me. You are a wonderful, loving daddy and husband. Your commitment and faithfulness to Christ despite all the trial and sickness you've suffered are an encouragement to me and to many others. My constant prayer is that God will heal you completely so that our little boys will have you to raise them to be faithful, godly men like you are.

Thank you so much for being strong for me these past months. Even when you were sick, you could say,

"God is with us, and I truly have peace and accept His will for our lives." I don't think I could have made it if I had seen you give up or get bitter. I'm so proud of you, of how strong you have been, of how good a daddy you are. You are a committed and loving husband and a dedicated Christian to the utmost.

My respect and love for you grow deeper every day. Thank you so much for trying to meet my needs and those of our boys too. I love you so and need you lots.

Love, your adoring wife, Nicole

Before leaving for another treatment, Donny sent out another email update.

Our six-week siesta is almost over. Our family has thrived with the little bit of normal living. We were able to go to church and plant a little garden. We will finish our time of rest this weekend with a stay at the Oregon coast. Nicole's mother rented a beach house for the whole family in celebration of Nicole's father's seventieth birthday.

Michelle sat alone on the beach, some distance from where Donny was playing with his boys when she heard an audible voice, "Enjoy this time together, for it will be the last time like this you have with Donny."

Startled, she looked around to see who was talking to her, but no one else was near. She was sitting alone in her spot on the sandy beach under cloudless skies. "Lord God, is this message from you?" she whispered as she looked up into the heavens and then again at the deserted beach surrounding her.

"No, Lord, don't tell me that! I'm not ready to hear it," she cried aloud. Pain gripped her as farther down the sandy stretch she heard Dallas and Dustin yelling, "Daddy, Daddy!" and saw their daddy running as he chased his sons.

"Lord, the boys need their daddy!" she cried as she watched the interaction. Was her mind playing tricks? But no, she hadn't even been thinking of Donny when the voice spoke! Without a doubt she knew God was preparing her for the coming sorrow.

The weekend together was bittersweet, for she could not share the message with anyone but her husband. But she took as many family pictures as she could, treasuring this moment when they were all together.

Donny's next email to friends read:

Soon after returning to Mexico, our good friends, Jason and Lavina Smith from Ohio, came to spend one week with us. We hadn't seen them since they helped to move us out to Oregon in February 2007. Joseph, their six-year-old, came along to play with Dallas, and do the boys ever play! The pool is a favorite place, and they are always asking, "Can we go swimming?" They ask to swim before lunch. They ask to swim after lunch. They ask to swim before supper, and they ask to swim after supper. Sometimes they even ask before breakfast!

Fabric stores are almost like a magnet to my wife. "Sweetheart! I declare you can smell them ten miles away!" I tease her. Jason became our wives' "human" shopping cart to haul back all the fabric on their first trip. For the second trip they had the clinic van take them.

On Monday I was off treatments, so we headed to Revolution Street and hopped in a taxi to—guess where? Another fabric store! My wife is a pro at it, believe me. When she enters the store, about two or three fabric cutters appear out of nowhere and stand with their yardsticks in one hand and big grins on their faces!

I had better explain. The fabric is not for Nicole, but for other people. The prices at home can't compare with these, so we've been hauling it home, within our luggage weight limit, and selling it. We've even hauled it to Florida. Lavina is taking this fabric to Ohio to sell for us. Every bit earned helps defray our costs here.

On Sunday we spent the morning reading the Bible and singing. Thank you, Lavina, for bringing materials for Sunday school class. That was a bright spot for Dallas.

On Wednesday our friends left us with a big hole of loneliness, but we, too, leave in a couple more days.

DADDY, ARE YOU SAD?

14

Revelation 10:11

August–November 2009

Donny's friends rejoiced to receive this positive update in September 2009.

August has been a wonderful, busy month at home. Canning, freezing, pickling . . . We are feeling quite peachy lately. We picked sixteen bushels of peaches from a neighbor's orchard for twenty-five cents a pound. We gave half to Gail and Michelle and ended up with ONLY eight bushels. That kept us busy this week.

Ever dream of perfect summer weather? Come visit Oregon! We spent some time camping in Mt. Hood National Forest. It is a twenty-minute drive from our house, and we love roughing it!

Yesterday we took a mini-vacation and visited Yaquina Head lighthouse. I was even able to walk up the circular stairway to see the beacon at the top! The prisms at the top are still original—120 years old!

The other day we found two "mud monsters" in our yard. After dousing them with water from the hose, we found they actually belonged to us!

Dallas had his fourth birthday on August 31, and Dustin turned two on September 7.

The continuous question around here is "Why?"

"Why are circles round?"

"Why is the sky blue?"

"Why are windows square?"

"Why is your dad called Dad, and I call him Grandpa?" On and on the questions go. I try to answer patiently because that's how a child learns, right?

Donny's fingers flew across the keys as he typed.

Sweet news! My October 16 report tells me that the leukemia is still in remission!

A week later he recorded a sacred experience in his personal journal.

My wife lay wrapped in slumber, but I could not go to sleep. When this happens, I use the time to talk with my Lord. I lie there, thinking of the future and praising God for once more allowing my body to heal.

Revelation 10:11, Revelation 10:11, Revelation 10:11— the reference kept popping up, interrupting my thoughts. I ignored the interference because I had no clue what the verse said, but it persisted in plaguing me. Finally I knew I couldn't ignore it any longer, and I got up. It was 12:38 a.m.

Taking my Bible into the bathroom, I looked up the reference and read: "And he said unto me, Thou must prophesy again before many peoples, and nations, and tongues, and kings."

I read it again. Wonder filled me. I felt God's presence surrounding me. I heard God saying in the stillness, "Donny, the road ahead will be rough and hard, but in the end it will be worth it all."

I can't describe the peace that filled the bathroom. It is beyond human comprehension. I have no words to tell you, but the peace I have within my soul gives me courage to go on. I went back to bed awed, knowing the Spirit of the Lord had spoken to me. I praise God that I heeded the Spirit's prompting.

A week passed before I could share God's revelation with my wife. I needed to ponder it. It was so sacred. I had to have time alone.

When Donny shared this experience with his wife and showed her the verse, Nicole felt as if her heart had dropped to the bottom of her stomach. Intense heartache engulfed her. Deep down she knew what God was telling her husband. *This will get worse, not better, before I give you a heavenly healing.*

"Sweetheart, God did not say I would die," Donny reminded her, trying to quiet her fears and her tears.

God knew the sorrow in Nicole's heart, and He had a gift of joy waiting for her. The following Sunday Donny and Nicole were taken in as members of the Porter church. Both had longed to take this step for some time, but with

Donny's treatments and health battles, their opportunities to attend services had been limited.

"Thank you, Lord for this church, your church, where truth is taught and the Gospel lived in the lives of your people. Use us in the furtherance of your kingdom and for your glory," Donny prayed.

In November, sickness swept through the community of Estacada. It did not bypass the Goods. The following letter went out.

It is November, a month since I wrote the last entry. Our family caught a severe virus that has given us bad head and chest colds. We make a pretty miserable lot! Everyone is weak, tired, and not very functional.

Fear grips me as I lie on the chair in the throes of a fever. It feels like a log truck hit me, and I have a horrible cough. "Lord, I'm afraid." I think of Dr. Rubio's words. "Donny, you are in remission, but if you should catch a virus, it could turn the leukemia back on."

Is this the beginning again? I dare not panic, for God is here. God is in control! God does answer prayer, and I remember Revelation 10:11. "God, my God, please heal each of us and especially keep your healing hand on me."

Pray for us.

Michelle grieved for Nicole as both families battled sickness. She longed to go help her sister, but her own family was sick. Newborn Josiah took much of her time. Each time her thoughts went to Nicole, they invariably back-tracked to the message God had given her at the beach. *Will this flu trigger the leukemia's return? How long will my sister have a husband?* Michelle wondered.

Newspaper headlines proclaimed a widespread swine flu epidemic. It swept not only across the United States but hit other countries as well. The flu would even close Mexico's borders, but before that happened, Donny would be at the clinic again.

DADDY, ARE YOU SAD?

15

Flu Virus

November 2009

Friday morning dawned, and Nicole knew her husband needed to return to the clinic. Since catching the flu virus, she had watched him go steadily downhill. This morning he had woken up deathly pale and drenched with sweat. The verse God had spoken to her husband flashed before her, but she pushed the revelation aside. She could not think of that right now. She needed to focus on her husband's needs.

She called her brother-in-law. "Gail, we have to go to Mexico. Donny's bad. We should be going right now."

Gail immediately took charge. "You start packing. I will get tickets and then be over to help you pack." He knew his sister-in-law was still recuperating from her own bout with the flu.

Nicole felt lightheaded and weak. Walking around in a daze, she threw together what she could think of. *How can I travel with two little boys feeling like this?* she wondered, but pushed the question into the background. Time was running out, and they had to leave.

Gail arrived with their tickets. With his help, everything was soon packed into the van, and they were on the way to the airport. Traffic slowed to a crawl before they reached the city, and Gail knew they would never make the flight unless it was late. When they pulled up to the airport, Gail knew he didn't have time to find a parking space. He would just have to drop them off at the entrance. He hated leaving the sick little family on their own, but there was nothing else for him to do.

"Take care of them, Lord," he pleaded as he watched an airport attendant wheel Donny away in a wheelchair while Nicole pushed the boys in their double stroller.

Nicole panicked when Donny was pushed though security and she was left behind with the bags and the boys. Weakness hit her in waves. Her mind wanted to blank out. *You must get to the gate! You must get to the gate!* she mentally repeated over and over, willing herself to move faster. It seemed her feet were refusing to cooperate, as though her body did not have the strength to do what she told it to do.

What a pathetic sight they made! She could see sympathy written on people's faces as she struggled on with the boys. Reaching the gate, she found her husband waiting, but the plane had left. So the ragtag little family, at the mercy of strangers, waited for the next flight to San Diego.

Our twentieth trip down for treatments! Nicole sighed as tears threatened to spill over. *If only we would have a direct flight instead of having to change planes. Our connecting flight will actually be our eightieth flight segment since we began these travels,* she thought wearily as she tried to pacify crying Dustin.

Before the little family got off the first plane to meet their connecting flight, God lovingly sent airport personnel to help them. Both Donny and Nicole were put in wheelchairs and escorted to their new gate while another attendant wheeled the stroller with the boys. Nicole felt as if she were in a nightmare. She kept praying for strength. She prayed continuously that her husband would live until they got to the clinic. God heard her request. At 2 a.m., they arrived at the clinic.

By this time Donny was so dehydrated they could not find a vein in his arm to insert the IV needle. An hour later, Nicole finally had time to give Gail and Michelle a call and let them know they had arrived. By the time she had finished leaving a phone message, the doctors had found a vein in Donny's foot, and Donny went to sleep.

Michelle saw the answering machine flashing at 3 a.m. She listened to her sister's strangled message, "Michelle, we are here. They are trying to get a vein. I am afraid Donny is going to die. He is really in bad shape. Why is God doing this to me? If Donny dies, I want to die. I'm afraid he will not make it through the night."

Gail and Michelle sat in their dark bedroom, listening to the message and crying for the suffering family. "Nicole, Nicole," Michelle cried, and her sister's pain once again became her pain.

On Saturday Gail and Michelle got another call from

Mexico. "They put a port in Donny's chest so he can receive more IVs. Both his hemoglobin and platelets are very low. He is too weak to walk, and he is coughing up foamy mucus," Nicole told them. "Pray for me. As soon as I hang up, I'm going to talk to the doctor to see what is going on."

"Dr. Rubio, please tell me what is going on," she pleaded, looking directly at the doctor. "I want to know. I need to know."

The doctor honored her request. "The foamy mucus is due to dehydration which is causing the lining of the lungs to start breaking down. His breathing difficulty comes from anoxia, due to oxygen starvation. The body begins to shut down when dehydration is severe. We have to be very careful how quickly we administer things, otherwise the body will simply reject them," he explained.

Nicole sat stunned, hearing mostly the words, "the body begins to shut down." Was her husband dying? Was his leukemia back?

Late Saturday Donny sent a brief email.

This evening I can breathe better. Mom and Dad Good are coming tomorrow. I am so tired and weak. This journey seems scary, but we are trying to keep our trust in God.

Then on November 18, his praying family and friends received more detailed information.

I can't express how we feel. I should have been dead today. But once again God has spared my life. He has a reason for me to live. The news is bittersweet, I guess you can say. Dr. Rubio told us the results from the blood work. I am in stable condition.

Tears stood in Dr. Rubio's eyes as he told us, "The virus you caught, Donny, did turn the leukemia back on." He seemed so sad.

"Donny," he simply said, "I'm only a doctor. I have my tools that I know to use. God is the healer, and I am only human. The only things I can offer at this point are the tools I know, which are higher-dose, more intense chemotherapy treatments."

"We want to pray about the situation," I answered. "We will give you an answer by the end of the week."

We are hit hard by this, and we want to question why. But at the same time, it is amazing what peace we feel in this situation. I am just amazed how we feel such a sense of God's presence.

Nicole is pretty weak and is still getting over her flu. She is also on IVs and improving, but the diagnosis is really hard on her.

Donny picked up his tablet and pen.

November 19 – Today I see a smile on my wife's face, and she is looking stronger emotionally. I think she is ready to fight this thing again. Praise the Lord! He is so good!

Last night she said, "Darling, every time this thing hits us I feel like I am knocked harder and harder. It is incredibly painful to watch your husband almost die again."

My wife is a wonderful woman. She is pulling herself together and is ready to fight the good fight of faith.

"For we wrestle not against flesh and blood, but against principalities, against powers, against the rulers of the darkness of this world, against spiritual wickedness in high places. Wherefore take unto you the whole armor of God, that ye may be able to withstand in the evil day, and having done all, to stand" (Ephesians 6:12–13).

The boys are doing okay now that Daddy is looking better. The first couple days Dallas would hardly even look at me and did not want to talk to me.

"Is Daddy going to die?" he asked Mommy.

When we were home this last time he said, "I'm so happy because Daddy is getting better!" He thought we would never have to go to Mexico again. Then this happened, and his world was blown apart.

Two days later Donny shared this:

Dr. Rubio was very understanding when we told him we have decided not to undergo more chemo. He is so caring and compassionate. I am grateful for his attitude. The staff is sad to see us go, but they all want the best for us.

Today we packed up and moved to a motel called the Dali Suites. It is a half mile from another clinic, called Hope4Cancer, where I will begin an enzyme therapy program. Our suite has an extra bed for Dallas and a full kitchen equipped with all cooking utensils. "Thank you, Lord, for providing this wonderful place to be as a family."

Mom and Dad Good extended their tickets for another week. When Dad got off the phone with Delta Air Lines, he said, "When I explained why we wanted our tickets extended, the agent waived the one-hundred-dollar change fee and said, 'Tell your son I am praying for him.' "

"Thank you, God, for your goodness. Thank you that we do not have to be alone at this time. You are so good!"

We feel peace in our decision. God is directing our lives, and it is amazing how things have fallen in place to move on to this new type of treatment. We don't know how we would have coped without my parents being here for us at this time.

The beach is right across the road. You guessed it! It is the boys' favorite spot to be! Oasis of Hope hospital is right around the corner. It is exactly two years since the leukemia returned for the second time and I came to Oasis for three weeks of treatments. Now I have left Rubio's, and I'm in the same neighborhood where I began.

Sometimes in life it feels as if you walk in circles.

On Sunday we joined Oasis for their Sunday morning worship service.

DADDY, ARE YOU SAD?

16

Hope4Cancer Institute

November 2009–January 2010

Once again, Donny and Nicole's friends rejoiced with them when they checked their mail and read:

> This is the day the world calls Black Friday, but I tell you, my friends, this Friday to me is beautiful, bright, and wonderful. I am alive! I am feeling good, and God has seen fit to spare my life again. Friends, don't ever take for granted a single day of your lives. Every day is a gift, given to you by God. Do something that you haven't done for a while. Look up, take a deep breath, smile, and say, "Thank you, God, for life."
>
> Thanksgiving Day was beautiful and sunny with 80-degree temperatures. We ate dinner at Oasis, and I'm afraid we pigged out! It was a traditional American Thanksgiving meal with the addition of an elaborate fresh vegetable tray and several kinds of fruit juice blends to sample. It was absolutely delicious!
>
> Let me explain what I am doing here at the clinic that seems to be helping. The program uses powerful enzymes that do not destroy your good cells. I am taking

all of these enzymes in pill form.

What is my leukemia count now? Dr. Tony Jimenez, the one who runs the clinic, will not take another test until the end of next week. He wants to give the enzymes time to work. He feels that a person's body is the best indicator of what is helping. As long as I am feeling well and improving, that is what he is most concerned about.

This morning I was walking to the clinic, the sun was shining, and I burst into song. "My Jesus knows just what I need; He satisfies, and every need supplies; Yes, He knows just what I need."

Because Daddy feels better, Dallas is positive and happy. Every day when I return from the clinic, he runs to me and gives me a big hug.

Nicole and I marvel at how we feel such peace and calm in our current situation. We are not living in a depressed black hole. "Thank you, God, for the prayers of our family and friends."

Jerry and Melrose are here with us again. They are staying for a week. I love having my family around! They brought Jevin, their 2½-year-old son, along. Our boys think it is wonderful to have a playmate!

On December 5 another letter went out.

With my platelets remaining very low, Dr. Tony wanted me to have a platelet transfusion. I preferred going back to Rubio's, as I had been getting them there for the last year and a half, and I am more comfortable knowing who my donor is.

"Where are Dallas and Dustin?" the staff wanted to know as they swarmed around me when I walked into Rubio's clinic. We ended up talking to friends and staying four hours!

When we finished up at Rubio's, we needed to get a taxi to take us back to the Dali Suites. The ride back takes twenty-five minutes, and as we neared our motel, I could see the meter. Taking my money from my pocket, I counted it. *Oh, no,* I thought, *I don't have enough. Now what am I going to do?* Right at that moment Nicole opened a card that one of our friends had given us that evening at Rubio's. Out fell a twenty-dollar bill!

"Lord, we thank you! Once again you have shown us that we are in your care! You have not forgotten us!"

My sweet wife has been fighting fears again since I needed the platelet transfusion. I am sure every caregiver understands some of these fears. "What if the program you are doing is not working? What if we just go back home, and it comes right back?" she asks me, not expecting an answer.

I remind her, "This is where God has led us. He has opened the door for us to come here. We do feel secure and have peace, but we must put our total trust in God." *If we were not here, where would we be?* I ask myself. If this is where God wants us to be, He will not let us down.

Since coming here, we have met patients from Canada, South Carolina, New York, Washington, Montana, Texas, and Australia. We have seen metastasized breast cancer, liver cancer, neuroblastoma cancer, brain cancer, pancreatic cancer, and ovarian cancer. Dr. Tony does not have 100 percent success, but so far every patient I have seen has responded well to the treatments. It is amazing to me because it is all being done without chemotherapy or radiation.

The personal atmosphere in the clinic is tremendous. Meal times last from one to two hours, and if conversations get interesting, you might start out with two or three people and end up with four or five more joining. When a patient leaves the clinic after being here for a week or two, it is a big event, with everyone standing at the door waving goodbye. Does God have a work for us here? Yes! I feel this in my heart.

A bad storm blew in on December 17 in the late afternoon. The wind blew at fifty to sixty miles per hour. Roofs blew off. Debris was flying everywhere. Then the power went out!

"Now what?" Nicole asked Donny as their room grew darker and darker. Donny shrugged, not having an answer either. Before many minutes passed, however, a knock sounded on their door, and the Dali Suites management handed them candles. Donny and Nicole decided to have a "romantic" candlelit supper with two excited boys! Dallas and Dustin were having so much fun that they didn't even want to turn the lights on when the electricity came on again at 8 p.m.!

Flipping open his tablet, Donny wrote:

Nicole was struggling badly this week with accepting our situation. She feared that the platelets had continued dropping. We had plans to fly home the twenty-second for Christmas. The possibility of NOT going home was pretty hard on her as well.

"Donny," she cried, "I don't understand! Last week I spent a lot of time in prayer asking God for peace in accepting the future. And I did receive God's peace! My fears were gone. So why am I back at the same place?" she wailed. I held her in my arms, trying to comfort her while praying to God to give me wisdom in helping her.

I knew what she said was true. I had watched her. I had seen the peace on her face. Then *SLAM!* The peace was gone. She has been in an intense battle the last five days. We prayed together. We cried to God to hear us and give divine peace, and still the battle raged.

Satan has a way of trying our most vulnerable areas. We must remember we fight not against flesh and blood, but against principalities, powers, and rulers of darkness.

But I rejoice to write here, "Thank you, Lord. My wife's peace has been restored—a peace which passes all understanding."

. . . .

Two weeks ago Dali Suites gave Dallas a floor mat to play on, but instead of playing on it, he took two chairs in our room, turned them over on top of the mat and covered them with a blanket. "This is my tent," he said, and he has slept in his "tent" ever since.

. . . .

Tonight at bedtime both boys were crying. Taking Dallas onto my lap, I cuddled him while Nicole held Dustin. "Tell Daddy why you are crying," I probed.

"I just want to go home! I want to sleep in my snowman bed," he sobbed, referring to his sheets with snowmen on them. He clung tighter to me. "I don't want you to get really sick again! If you get really sick, we can't go home for Christmas!"

Nicole and I looked at each other with tears running down our cheeks. We held our children closer, our tears and heartbreak mingling with theirs.

Although Donny and Nicole and the boys had to stay in Mexico over Christmas, there was a bright spot. Gail and Michelle and their family came to spend Christmas with them. The children were delighted to have playmates, and Donny and Nicole were thrilled with the presence of their guests. The clinic was closed on Christmas Day for some remodeling, but Donny was able to continue his therapies that day at the Dali.

Gail and Michelle and their family were able to have a room upstairs close to Donny and Nicole's room. Once the children were sleeping for the night, the couples made tea and popcorn to share together on the stair steps.

"I love this safe environment with the enclosed courtyard," Michelle confided as they enjoyed the quiet time together. But the next day Michelle felt anything but safe.

"We think our van was stolen," Gail informed his wife.

"It can't be!" Michelle was incredulous. But when she went outside, it was not there.

"But it's broad daylight!" she sputtered as reality settled in. "To think our van was stolen right off the street during the day!"

"When Gail and I went outside to move the van and discovered it was gone," Donny said, "we stood there dumbfounded! We could not believe it! What makes it more ironic is that when we were at Oasis today, Bruce Northy, who is from Wisconsin and volunteering there, asked me, 'How long is your brother-in-law staying at the Dali?'

" 'The rest of the week,' I answered.

" 'Well,' he said, 'why don't you park the van here at Oasis behind the fence? Dali has no protection and a number of times the parked vehicles have been stolen. You had better move it before tonight.' I thanked him and assured him we would.

"Now this! In broad daylight! Unbelievable! It is only 4:30 in the afternoon." Donny shook his head.

"Tomorrow we have to go downtown and file a police report," Gail said, taking up the story. "I doubt it will do much good though, because in talking to people around here, they say our van is history unless God performs a miracle."

DADDY, ARE YOU SAD?

"What did you have in it? Anything valuable?" Nicole questioned.

"Thankfully not much. All we left in it were the children's car seats."

One day the two families decided to take the bus to downtown Tijuana and do a little shopping. When they got off the bus, the men were getting the children's strollers ready when suddenly a big man walked right up to Donny and asked in English.

"What are your children talking about?"

"I don't know. I wasn't listening," Donny answered, smelling the liquor on the man's breath. *Oh, no, a drunk,* he thought. The man then gave him a gang-style handshake— shaking his hand, clasping his fingers, and then bumping Donny's hand with his fist. After the man bumped Donny's fist, he then reared back and slammed Donny's fist really hard.

Oh, no! This man is drunk and strong! Donny thought in dismay.

The man then looked at Nicole, saying, "Look at those blue eyes; look at those pretty blue eyes." Donny tried to stand between them, but the man kept moving, trying to look Nicole in the eyes.

As they hurried to get their things together, Donny told Nicole, "Go on ahead with Gail's family, and I will stay between you and this man."

Nicole went ahead down the sidewalk. Before Donny could get started, the man got close to the faces of Dallas and Dustin in the stroller and said, "Oh, look at those blue eyes; you've got pretty blue eyes." He crouched down so he could stare into their eyes. Donny quickly took the stroller and started down the sidewalk, hoping the man would not follow, but sure enough, he did.

"I'm not following you. This is the way I'm going," he kept hollering every time Donny looked back. Finally the two families turned into a store, hoping the man would move on. The rest went inside while Donny stayed between them and the man. Again the man called out, "This is the way I'm going. I am not following you," while he stood staring right at Donny.

Donny wanted to enjoy their outing and finally got up courage to suggest, "Well, if that is the way you are going, then please go," and pointed down the street.

This made the man instantly angry. Letting loose a shipload of profanity, he ranted, "You are the ones in my country! You are the ones who need to leave! I am Mexican! You are American! I have no need of you. You came to my country. I did not ask you to come. You have to leave now!"

"We are leaving, sir," Donny answered, wishing he had kept his mouth shut.

"Leave now!" came the belligerent order.

"We are leaving, sir," Donny assured him.

Suddenly the man changed his tune and said, "I'm going to leave. You stay right here and don't move. I'm going right down this sidewalk, and you don't move," he kept repeating.

Amazingly, the man did leave. Once he was out of sight, the two families left the store, crossed the street, and headed in the opposite direction.

"Weren't you scared?" Michelle asked.

"No," Donny could answer honestly. "I didn't feel fear because God tells us that He has not given us the spirit of fear, but of power, and of love, and of a sound mind. This man had the power of Satan in him, and I knew God is more powerful. Also, I have a sound mind, and the man did not act as if he did. I felt as though I were battling the devil, though, more than battling a drunk. I actually felt sorry for the man," Donny said. "He showed so much anger. I wonder what all has happened in his life."

That evening Dustin lay around holding his blanket. He had been acting normal all day, so Donny and Nicole were puzzled. They felt his forehead. He was warm and starting to get a fever. Suddenly Dustin started twitching and throwing himself around.

"Is he having a seizure?" Nicole grew frantic, but when they talked to him, he smiled and made noises. For a couple of hours until bedtime that was all Dustin did. He lay on the bed, twitched and threw himself around. The parents kept close watch on the fever, but it never got very high.

"I don't think we should put him in the crib if he's acting like this." Donny voiced his concern at his son's abnormal actions. "Do you think we should take him to the hospital? What if he stops breathing?"

"I don't know what we should do," Nicole replied, just

as puzzled. "I don't want to bother Gail and Michelle, as their children will be sleeping by now. But he has been acting so strange ever since we got back from shopping."

"Let's pray." Donny reached for his wife's hand, and they poured out their concerns to God—their source of help.

"Show us what to do, Lord," Donny prayed. "We need your wisdom. Fear wants to take hold since we don't understand what is happening. We ask that your will be done in this situation."

"Nicole," Donny said after a bit, "I think the devil wants us to have this fear. Instead of fear, we need to come to Jesus." The parents laid their hands on their little son and Donny prayed again, "God, our heavenly Father, we come to you in this hour of need. Thank you that your power is greater than the powers of evil and darkness that surround us. We ask for your healing touch upon our son. In the name of Jesus, remove the power of evil that wants to harm him. Thank you that we can claim you as Lord and Saviour of our lives. In Jesus' name, Amen."

Peace came over Donny and Nicole as they laid Dustin into his bed, and soon they fell into a restful sleep.

Dustin slept well all night, and the next morning his fever was gone. He acted totally normal and showed no sign or symptom of getting sick, or of anything having been wrong.

Had the man cast an evil spirit on Dustin? Why did he want to look the boys in the eyes? It was a question they could not answer, but they did know that God's power was available to His children. They did believe that God wanted them to put their faith into practice and trust in their all-powerful God.

"Thank you, God. Because of your Son, Jesus, we can be free from the spirit of fear." Rejoicing filled their hearts.

. . . .

Several nights after Gail's van was stolen, Nicole and Donny were sound asleep.

Suddenly they were startled awake by a terrifying bang that sounded like a gunshot. They lay like frozen statues under their covers, feeling that even their breathing was too loud. A moment before, they had been warm and cozy; now it felt as though the temperature had suddenly dropped about twenty degrees, causing goose bumps too numerous to count. Feeling as if his hair stood on end, Donny peeked out from under the covers and looked at the clock: 3:45 a.m.

In a voice barely audible, Nicole whispered, "What was that?"

"I don't know," her husband whispered back.

"Can you go look out the window and see?" she wondered.

"No," came the whispered reply. "You go look out the window!"

"Okay," Nicole consented. "I'll look out the window if you lock the deadbolt on the door."

"I guess," came Donny's reluctant consent. There was not

much else to say if his wife was brave enough to look out the window! Stealthily the two crept out of bed, imagining that any minute the door would come bursting open. Very quickly and quietly, the deadbolt on their door slid into place while Nicole peeked out the window.

"I don't see anything," she said. Donny took his turn at the window and didn't see anything either. Quickly getting under the covers, they both listened for another sound, but all was silent. Sleep eventually came, but the next morning as Nicole got out of bed, she felt something cold and rubbery under her bare foot. Laughter filled the room when she realized she was standing on two popped balloons! The mystery of the night had been solved!

During Gail and Michelle's visit, Donny sent out this email:

On New Year's Day we went to the ocean and got "cocos." Let me explain. When you buy a coconut in the store in the States, all you see is a hard brown outer shell with the white meat of the coconut inside. Down here you get the whole thing! Straight off the tree, the coconuts have a thick green outer shell and an inside hard brown shell. When you buy one here to eat, they first cut a hole in the top and you drink out the coconut milk. This is extremely nutritious. Then you give it back and they cut it in half, loosen the coconut meat, cut it in pieces, and you squeeze lime juice onto it and sprinkle salt all over it. Mmm! Yummy!

Dallas and Dustin are having the time of their lives with

cousins to play with. Dallas knows they will soon be leaving and keeps asking, "Is it Sunday now?" He is scared that each day is the last.

It has been wonderful for my wife to have her twin here. It was good for both of us to have family with us over the holidays. I marvel at the strength and courage Nicole shows every day. Yes, she has her times of discouragement, but after a good cry, she picks herself up, asks God for strength, and goes on.

"Lord, give our friends joy to fill their days, peace to fill their hearts, and love to fill their lives as they begin a new year."

"For I know the thoughts that I think toward you, saith the LORD, thoughts of peace, and not of evil, to give you an expected end" (Jeremiah 29:11).

Our parting was almost too painful to put in words, Michelle penned in her diary as they left Mexico. *Have you ever hugged your sister when it felt like a sharp knife blade was piercing, twisting its jagged edges into every recess of your insides until you thought it was impossible to endure? Have you ever held your sister, or brother-in-law, and felt them tremble with grief at parting, or felt two crying little boys clinging to you, not wanting your family to leave? Have you ever had to be strong when your heart felt like it was breaking in a million pieces? Lord God, it is so hard, but we leave our dear ones in your keeping.* She ended her entry, blinking away the tears.

Gail's family was waiting to cross the border back into the

United States. As the vehicle they were in sat in the long line of traffic, Michelle could no longer keep from asking the question burning in her mind. "Gail, how much longer will this go on? How much longer can they handle this trauma?" she asked quietly as tears threatened to flow again.

She could not erase the picture of the forlorn little family standing in front of the Dali Suites, bravely waving goodbye.

"I don't know how much longer," Gail answered slowly. He, too, was thinking of the sadness etched on the faces of their loved ones. "We must pray earnestly for them. They are so courageous!"

"I know," his wife was quick to agree. "A person can see Donny is suffering. He is wasting away from nausea. Who knows what other pain he lives with, but he is slow to complain and wears a perpetual smile. It's no wonder people gravitate to him!"

Slowly their driver inched his way through the sea of vehicles headed toward the United States border inspection station. "I haven't been through many border crossings, but each time we come through here I am amazed. This traffic is unreal!" Gail shook his head as he tried to count how many lanes of traffic they were in. "I've counted twelve lanes on our side of the barrier, and it looks like the same amount on the other side. Twenty-four lanes all headed in the same direction! No wonder it is considered the world's busiest port of entry!"

Once the driver pulled away from the border station,

it did not take long for traffic to speed up. The road kept narrowing until they were down to normal lanes.

"Now, all we need to do is pick up a van at the car rental agency, and we will be ready to drive home." Gail gave a yawn as he thought of the many miles to cover before they were home.

Two hours later they were cruising up Interstate 5. The children had fallen asleep. In the quietness, Michelle's thoughts returned to the conversation she and Gail had had prior to the border crossing.

"Honey, I will never forget Donny's talk on Sunday morning at Oasis. At least, I hope I will always remember it," she added.

"I know," her husband replied after a bit, and Michelle knew he was deep in thought.

"Care to share what you are thinking?" his wife probed. "We have twenty-one hours of driving, and I am listening!"

"Are you sure?" he teased, and then his tone became serious. "I'll start by telling you what Donny told me. It still sends a shiver through me when I think about it.

" 'Have you ever had God speak to you?' Donny asked me. Then he said, 'I have, but I'm not sure I can really explain what happened.' His face lit up then as he related this happening.

" 'One night, the last time we were home, I was lying in bed unable to sleep, and the reference, Revelation 10:11, would not leave my mind. I did not know what the verse said, so I kept dismissing it until I wondered,

Is God trying to tell me something?

" 'I went into the bathroom with my Bible so I would not disturb Nicole, and I turned to the verse. Gail,' he said, looking at me with a glow that radiated from within, 'when I read the verse, something happened! I can't describe what, but something happened to me. I knew God was in our little bathroom right beside me. I felt God's holy presence. What I felt was a living presence, but I was by myself. I was surrounded by holiness, but I don't have any words to explain what it was like. I only know God was with me. God told me, "I have a mission yet for you to do." He said it would not be easy, but in the end it would be worth it all.' "

As Michelle listened to the narrative, she sat in awe of the marvelous workings of God. The earth was filled with humans. There were scores of hurting, suffering people in the world, yet God cared enough about each of them individually to reveal Himself in a very personal way. She hugged her thoughts to herself. She, too, could testify to hearing God's audible voice and the wonder of it!

"What is the verse in Revelation?" she broke the silence to ask.

"Thou must prophesy again before many peoples, and nations, and tongues, and kings."

"Gail!" she exclaimed as her heart hammered with realization. "Donny is doing that very thing! People come from various states and countries, and they speak other languages! No wonder he spends every hour he can in ministering to others! He is fulfilling the mission God laid out for him."

"After Donny shared this experience, things became clear to me." Gail paused, and his wife raised one eyebrow in question. "I had been concerned that he was pushing himself too hard. I thought he should be resting more instead of constantly singing and ministering spiritually to the patients. 'You are sick yourself!' I wanted to tell him. 'Don't do so much, or you will wear yourself down again!' But I didn't say anything.

"I would hear Donny ask patients, 'Can I pray for you?' when he saw them battling depression or discouragement. Patients would nod in agreement. Then Donny would not only pray, but he would go on to share his testimony of what God means to him. He never left them until they were aware that God loves them too.

" 'I want every person I make contact with to understand the need of having a personal, saving relationship with God,' Donny emphasized, and he is certainly trying to make sure that happens."

Michelle wiped her tears. "I didn't know all this. What else do you know?"

"I don't think I ever told you what Dr. Tony said, did I? Dr. Tony said he loves to get a roomful of patients who are feeling down, ready to give up and bitter at life, and have Donny go talk to them. The effect is amazing! They listen! They weep as he tells his story of God's goodness to him, and how someday he will be healed forever. Donny speaks from his heart. He shares Bible verses and prays for them.

"Dr. Tony said his patients leave with a different outlook because Donny has left them with hope. The doctor has seen amazing results of healing in their lives because of the way God is using Donny to encourage them."

Surely, Michelle thought as she digested all her husband had shared, *Surely God won't let Donny die, will He? Not when he is doing so much for his Lord?* But she remembered the voice on the beach, and her heart bled at what she felt certain was coming.

DADDY, ARE YOU SAD?

17

Testing and Faithfulness

January–April 2010

Friends wept tears of helplessness when they read this letter from Donny:

January 9, 2010 – I have been having fevers off and on again. Another issue to contend with is pain in my left hip. This is not a shooting pain, but more like a charley-horse pain. It got so bad Tuesday and Wednesday that with the pain and the fevers, I was writhing in bed.

Dr. Tony wonders if the port in my chest is infected, or if my condition has something to do with the hip?

I had a good talk with him, and it looks as if we will be down here for the long haul, at least another six weeks or so. My body is at a place where I dare not do anything to tip it over the edge. It is warm and sunny here, and I can get out and walk, which is very healing for me. Even though we miss everyone at home, we are willing to stick it out here if this is where I am to be.

Nicole's parents came and spent ten days with us. They came at a time when we badly needed them. Though this is only the second time they have come to Mexico, they have been a very strong support to us. Mom Smallfoot took on another job to further aid our family. Where would we be without them? "Thank you, Lord, for caring in-laws."

Dee found the time they spent with their children and grandchildren to be filled with happiness, yet underlining that joy was a heart-wrenching sadness. She saw Donny fighting for life. She observed her daughter joining his battle. The pain she and Floyd had experienced when Donny called with the first diagnosis grew sharper as they watched this daily suffering.

In spite of his illness, however, they could see that their son-in-law was busy sharing God's love to those he came in contact with. When Dee and Floyd left for home, they felt blessed and challenged to know that Donny's life reflected no bitterness but that he was magnifying the goodness of the God he served.

Donny's next email was sent January 24:

The pain has left my leg! They could find no reason for my leg pain, yet the last while I have been on pain medicine for it. Friday and Saturday I needed it every six hours, but on Sunday there was no pain! Let me tell you exactly when the pain left.

I began doing research about emotional issues that cause physical symptoms in the body. This made me curious. Could the pain in my leg be due to an emotional issue I was dealing with?

I thought of a talk that Dr. Francisco Contrarez gave on Thanksgiving Day about Jonah and the whale and how similar Jonah's story is to ours. Sometimes when God asks us to go through difficult things, we also try to run away. When Jonah was in the belly of the whale, he realized that God was giving him a chance to make things right. Jonah prayed, "But I will sacrifice unto thee with the voice of thanksgiving; I will pay that that I have vowed. Salvation is of the Lord" (Jonah 2:9).

Jonah prayed a prayer of thanksgiving! Jonah did not know God would spare his life, yet he thanked God for the situation he was in. Dr. Contrarez left us with a challenge, "Have you thanked God for your 'Nineveh' situation?"

Then it hit me. I have never truly thanked God for my situation! I have thanked God for all He has done, for the miracles, for sparing my life, for friends and church support, for all the good things He has blessed our family with, for answered prayer . . . but I had never thanked Him for my "Nineveh" situation.

I felt convicted. I felt I needed to thank God even though I did not know the outcome of my story. So I did. Since the day I began thanking God for my situation, the leg pain has been gone.

Do our emotions produce physical symptoms? I don't know a lot about that, but I believe God reminded me of Dr. Contrarez's message because He wanted me to possess a truly thankful heart.

My wife does so well in taking care of our family! Our

little kitchen has a small motel refrigerator and a two-burner stove which limits what kinds of foods she can prepare. We have beans, rice, and salad . . . salad, rice, and beans . . . rice, salad, and beans . . . rice and beans in tortillas . . . beans and rice in tortillas . . . but there are only so many things you can do on a stovetop! I do admire her creativity and determination to feed her family well.

Dallas and Dustin are getting a little housebound. Rain and wind with the power off and on has them learning to play doctor pretty well. The other night in bed, Dallas asked, "Daddy, are your lymphocytes leveling out?" Little ears hear more than you realize!

Nicole woke one Friday morning to find her husband in the throes of a severe allergic reaction to some of the enzyme treatments. The day before, Donny had had a reaction too, but as soon as he took a hot shower, the shakes stopped. Today the shower did not help, and unknown to Nicole, his body was going into anaphylactic shock. Still shaking and feeling nauseated, Donny crawled back into bed, piled on the blankets, and went back to sleep.

"Sweetheart, bring me ice-cold water," he requested when he woke up. "I am terribly thirsty." Nicole had taken him water several times when he asked, "Could you please get colder water?" Then Donny went back to sleep.

Is something wrong? Nicole wondered. To double-check, she took his pulse and found that his heart was racing. The best she could count, his heart rate was 150 beats per minute!

"Donny, wake up! I think we need to call the clinic." Nicole shook her husband in alarm. She breathed with relief when he woke up and said, "I'll send an email to Dr. Tony."

Reading the email he wrote sent warning bells pulsating through her. "Donny, this is totally unreadable!" she blurted out, but he got defensive.

"It's because my eyes don't focus right, and I see white spots," he answered and sent the email anyway.

When the office personnel got Donny's email, they sent someone right away to take Donny to the clinic. Nicole's apprehension grew when her husband could hardly walk, and the clinic staff almost carried him. *He is worse today,* she realized, blaming his symptoms on a reaction. But with the doctors taking care of her husband, Nicole put her worry aside. Besides, it was naptime, and she needed to put the boys to sleep.

Two hours later the boys woke up, and Nicole took them to the clinic to see Donny. She was shocked when a doctor met her at the door and said, "We just got Donny stabilized. We will know in an hour and a half whether he will make it or not."

She couldn't believe what she was hearing. She needed to see Donny! She needed to see him right now! In her shock, she forgot all about her little boys. Crippling fear made it almost impossible to walk, but she did make it to Donny's room, where she found him lying in bed, staring up at the ceiling with his eyes wide open.

Taking a deep breath to calm her pounding heart, she asked, "What happened, Donny? Do you know what happened?"

"I don't know," came his weak response, and Nicole sank into the chair beside his bed. *He is alive!*

It was amazing to Nicole how the other patients entertained her boys so she could stay with her husband. The doctors had given Donny a steroid injection, and ever so slowly the fever began dropping.

One week after this episode, Donny wrote this letter:

I don't remember going to the clinic. I don't remember Nicole talking to me. I don't remember her repeating Psalm 118:17.

"It was the only verse I could think to cling to," my wife told me later. The verse she kept repeating was, "I shall not die, but live, and declare the works of the Lord."

"Donny, I repeated the promise over and over to you. It wasn't just for you; it was for me too," she explained.

I don't remember Nicole feeding me supper. I don't remember talking to my parents. My memory started returning around 9 p.m., and I asked Nicole, "Did you just get here?" Of course she had been there all day, but each time she left the room and returned, I asked her the same question, and she would remind me she had been with me all day.

We spent the night at the clinic so I could be monitored to ensure that the fever would not return. Needless to say, my poor wife did not get much rest as I kept asking her questions. My memory and motor skills were still very unstable.

On Sunday I was very weak but more aware of things. Danny Wolfenbarger, Nicole's cousin who had spent a year in Ohio with us when I was first diagnosed, arrived at 4:30 that afternoon, and we returned to the Dali Suites.

A week later we welcomed a wonderful surprise!

A knock sounded on our door. We opened it and could not believe our eyes! Sam Eigsti from Buffalo, Missouri, stood grinning outside our door! He is a very good friend of ours whom we met over at Dr. Rubio's clinic. His wife had lymphoma and passed away two years ago this past September. He has seven children, and this is the first time he has gone anywhere by himself since her death. To think he came to spend the weekend with us! We were touched!

"I wanted to be a help and encouragement to you," he shared. And his surprise visit was certainly that. We had a good time and were sad to see him go home on Monday afternoon.

"It took a lot of courage for Sam to come back down to Mexico alone." I voiced our thoughts as I took my wife's hand, glad I was able to hold it.

"Lord, you are so good to us. Thank you for friends who care and who give us their time and support. Thank you, Lord, for sparing my life. We will simply enjoy each day you give us."

No one is ever guaranteed life from one day to the next.

Dear friends, take time to tell someone special you love them . . . take time to enjoy the fragrance of a flower . . . take time to realize there is a God who loves you.

In February, Delbert and Melissa Derstine from North Carolina surprised Donny and Nicole with a short visit. The two families had gotten acquainted by telephone and email when Melissa was diagnosed a year and a half earlier with cancer. The Derstines had come for treatments at another clinic in Mexico and used this opportunity to meet the Goods in person. Donny and Nicole found it a tremendous encouragement to visit with another couple walking through the same valley they were.

And it was a real encouragement to have Danny with them again. One evening Danny entertained the boys while Donny watched. Beside him lay his tablet. He picked it up. Slowly he opened it. Instead of writing, he bowed his head and closed his eyes. Sometime later, he again watched Danny still hard at play, but this time he smiled as he began writing.

I am jealous of you, Danny! I can tell the boys really latch onto you as a male role model as you play with them. I want to start a pity party for myself. I want to feel upset at life for its unfairness! I want to be a normal father with health and strength. I want to be giving my boys piggyback rides instead of watching you give them. I want my boys to play normal make-believe games instead of games about cancer and chemo. I want . . . but then a favorite verse comes to mind, ". . . be not dismayed; for I am thy God. I will strengthen thee; yea, I will help thee; yea, I will uphold thee with the right hand of my righteousness" (Isaiah 41:10).

I change my tune! I am jealous no more! I have so much! God is on my side! "Thank you, Lord, for sending Danny to us again. I do not know what we would do without him. I love him like a brother!"

"Incredible!" Danny breathed the word to himself as he watched Donny's interaction with the people they rubbed shoulders with each day. Donny's ability to empathize with those suffering life-threatening illnesses moved him to tears.

"How do you do it?" Danny questioned. "You aren't feeling well, yet when you ministered to the needs of others today, you acted alive. You seemed as though nothing were wrong with you! I've noticed it over and over again." As Danny waited for Donny to answer, he thought about the tremendous change that had taken place in Donny in the four years since he had lived with them in Ohio. He was amazed by the spiritual growth he saw in Donny.

"It may seem hard to believe, but when I am sharing God's love with others, I feel well, 100 percent well! I feel vibrant! I feel whole! I'm doing the work God called me to! It can only be the power of God that enables me to do this, Danny." As he spoke, Donny's face reflected the love and peace of his heavenly Father.

Danny felt God wanted him to stay at the clinic with Donny and Nicole as long as he was needed. This was where God had called him to serve. He was able to help with the daily needs of the boys and Nicole and offer support to Donny.

In April, Donny borrowed Danny's computer to send a long-overdue update.

My computer was sabotaged! Dustin is the guilty person, but we forgive him, as he did not know a cup of water would "fry" a computer for Daddy. The computer is across the border being repaired, so thanks to Danny, I am using a borrowed computer until ours is returned.

A molar I had pulled weeks ago is the biggest problem I have been dealing with now. I had a root canal done in 2004, and we have been waiting to have the tooth extracted for the last two years. X-rays showed I have a lot of infection under the roots and in the jawbone. I wanted to resume relatively good health first, but that has not happened. Dr. Tony and I decided maybe we should go ahead and do it now, to give my body help in healing.

It had been six weeks since I had a blood test done. We needed a current one to make sure all was okay. The results gave us a big surprise! Dr. Tony did not expect to see the hemoglobin down to 4.5. It has never been that low even when I came down in November at death's door. My white blood cell count was all the way up to 34, higher than at any time in the entire four years since my diagnosis.

"Most times I see counts like this when people are very, very sick. It is hard to believe the results with how you look and act," the doctor said.

I knew I was anemic due to the paleness of my hands and face. Also, whenever I exerted any kind of energy like walking or getting up too fast, I could feel my heart pounding, but we would never have guessed I was that anemic!

"I can't let fear rule me," I told Dr. Tony after we discussed what to do. "I have been feeling better, and I would rather focus on that than on numbers."

I needed five blood transfusions before the three-hour procedure of removing the tooth and scraping the infection out of the root cavities and the jawbone underneath. I am experiencing a lot of pain now because some of the infection was close to the nerve that runs along the bottom of the jaw. At night I have to keep my head propped on pillows; otherwise it feels like the blood is all rushing to my head. I cannot get a decent night of sleep. We taped a Bible verse on the wall that says:

"For I will restore health unto thee, and I will heal thee of thy wounds, saith the Lord" (Jeremiah 30:17).

DADDY, ARE YOU SAD?

18

Medical Friends

Staying at the clinic for months helped Donny and Nicole develop close relationships with the medical personnel, especially with Dr. Tony. Not only was he Donny's doctor, he was also his good friend. In Dr. Tony's free moments, he and Donny could often be found in deep discussion. "Your husband's knowledge of health and his faith in God fascinate me," Dr. Tony told Nicole.

When they would leave their prognosis meetings, Dr. Tony would give Donny a hug and say, "I love your family. Now remember, Donny, be good!" and Donny would reply, "I love you too."

Nicole cherished one particular incident she had witnessed. It had been late in the day when they made it to their scheduled appointment. Before their meeting had even begun, they both sensed Dr. Tony's discouragement. "It has been a hard day," he said apologetically as he rested his chin in his hand, his words threaded with weariness.

When they finished their meeting, Donny asked Dr. Tony if he could pray with him. He put his hand on the doctor's shoulder and prayed, "Lord God, bless Dr. Tony with wisdom and a healing touch as he gives his life to bring healing to our bodies." Tears stood in Dr. Tony's eyes. He was deeply touched by Donny's compassion, and the prayer served to strengthen the bond growing between the two men.

Another staff member everyone loved was the American representative, Pam. Pam had a friendly, positive attitude that endeared her to all. She had lost a parent to cancer and showed deep compassion to the patients. Pam's work involved resolving issues and communication problems between patients and the Mexican staff.

Then there was Alma, who had the opposite disposition. Alma worked in billing. She tended to be strict and enforce rules without much compassion. Most of the patients disliked her or were intimidated by her. But Donny won Alma over and started calling her his "Mexican Mama." She, in turn, ended up worrying over him and loving him like a son.

"How is my son today?" Alma would ask. She did everything possible to make life easier for the Good family.

Their clinic driver, Jesús, developed a special spot in his heart for the family. Jesús did errands for them, took them wherever they wanted to go, loved the boys, went out of his way to make things easier for them, and would never let them pay taxi fare. "This is what I want to do for you," he would say as he refused payment.

And then there was Gloria who worked at the front desk. She was a sweet, absent-minded girl whom they had to constantly remind about things she should have remembered. But everyone loved her anyway.

As Nicole's mind jumped from one staff member to another, she thought of her cousin Danny. *He's not one of the staff, but faithful Danny is in Mexico for as long as we need him! What would I do without my cousin?* Nicole wondered.

Thinking of Danny brought back yesterday's conversation and the much-needed encouragement he had given her. "Your husband has a tremendous influence on everyone he comes in contact with," Danny had told her.

"When I went with him to Rubio's for his blood transfusion, Donny suggested we drop in to see an old friend. You probably know her; she is in her sixties and isn't doing too well with her cancer. Anyway, we went into her room. It was dark, and she was lying in bed with the drapes closed. You could feel the heaviness, the depression, and the despair filling the room, but Donny walked over to her bed and knelt down without saying a word.

"I saw the woman and Donny just looking at each other. Soon they were crying together! I stood in the background with tears running down my own face, feeling a powerful moment of God's nearness.

"Then Donny quietly began quoting his favorite verse from Isaiah, 'Fear thou not; for I am with thee: be not dismayed; for I am thy God . . .' Nicole, I could see the array of emotions the woman was struggling with, and then the change as she listened to Donny share comfort from the Word of God.

"After encouraging her spiritually, he encouraged her to do as much as she could to improve her health. 'We are to take care of our bodies, even if God gives us life for only another day or week or month,' Donny told her.

"We ended up singing a few songs from our songbook, and as we left, you could see a real transformation! Her face showed the light of hope! The change in this woman is the same thing I have witnessed again and again as Donny reaches out.

"When Donny speaks at chapel, people gravitate to him afterward, because they feel his empathy. 'Can you come to my room?' they ask, and another door is opened to share God's love and hope. We sing for someone, and before we are done, people congregate in the hall to listen, and another door is opened. That happened last night. People here are hurting, and what Donny has to offer them leaves a profound impact."

Tears had glistened in Nicole's eyes as she listened. She knew that through everything they had experienced, difficult as it had been, both she and Donny had changed. God had used these experiences to shape and mold them, and they were not the same people Danny had known when he lived with them in Ohio.

19

Last Weeks in Mexico

April–May 2010

"Earthquake! Quick! Hurry! We have to get out of here!" The Goods' Sunday afternoon nap abruptly ended when Danny burst into their room to arouse them. In a drowsy trance, they fumblingly picked up the boys and headed outside as they felt the building ripple like a slow-motion roller coaster.

Neither Donny nor Nicole had ever experienced an earthquake, and it was fascinating to stand outside and see the vertical blinds on all five floors of the building swaying in unison with the trees. It was also a bit disconcerting.

Fifteen minutes after they had gone outside, everything was still, and they were able to go back inside. Later that afternoon, however, another tremor passed through like a galloping horse. One hundred miles north in South Baja, California, the earthquake's magnitude measured around 7.2. Several more aftershocks were also felt but not by the Good family. They were sound asleep!

The next evening Donny was admitted to the clinic for observation. To pass the time he sent out this short letter.

I started having reactions again, so we are at the clinic tonight. The reactions remind us so much of the time back in January. The doctors are puzzled as to what is causing the chills, fevers, and shakes to recur. "We don't understand what is happening," the medical personnel say.

But I tell them, "God says in Proverbs 3, 'Trust in the Lord with all thine heart; and lean not unto thine own understanding.' God does not expect us to always know and understand. God just wants us to trust in Him."

Donny then added this message in his journal.

O God, my God, I am so very weary. Hold my sweet wife in your arms when she gets faint. Give her strength, Lord, and thank you for being so good.

My Lord and God, I have a burning desire to share your message of salvation with everyone I meet. Give me strength and fill me with your wisdom. Help me, Lord, to use every opportunity for you.

Back in Oregon, Michelle looked at the clock. Eleven o'clock. She was glad Gail lay sleeping, but she could not go to sleep. Heaviness enveloped her as she thought of her sister's phone call earlier that afternoon.

"Michelle, life is so hard! I struggle in submitting to what God has called my husband to do. I know what he is doing for God is right, and I want him to witness to people and encourage them, but I long for a normal life! I hardly see him! He spends hours at the clinic. He is so weak and sick! He comes home exhausted, sometimes hardly able to walk.

"Oh, Michelle, it breaks my heart! His face glows with love; he is excited to be serving the Lord! Oh, I hardly know what I am saying!" Nicole cried out.

"Families staying here wait in the courtyard for him to return from the clinic so they can ask him questions or just talk to him. And he does talk to them! Pray for me. I am so mixed up inside. I just want my husband!

"I don't think Donny is improving. I think he is getting weaker. We are in the clinic again. It makes me feel horrible to struggle with submitting to this when my sick husband is touching lives for Christ. People I don't know thank me for sharing my husband with them.

"Just pray, Michelle. I do have peace in my heart, but Satan keeps tempting me."

Tears coursed down Michelle's cheeks as she lay in bed weeping for her sister, praying earnestly for her, beseeching God to let Nicole feel His loving arms around her. Michelle's heart pounded from the heavy, agonizing pain ripping through her. *Lord God, are you with us? We need you! This suffering is almost more than I can bear!* She wept silently, not wanting to awaken her weary, sleeping husband. The night seemed extra dark and silent. The burden she felt would not dissipate, so Michelle struggled on in prayer for her loved ones.

Suddenly, something startled her and her eyes flew open. Their room was no longer dark but filled with a soft glow.

Her eyes opened wider as she saw a human-like form of light enter the open bedroom door and look straight into her face. Sadness, yet compassion, flowed from the eyes as the form drifted over to her. She felt her heavy burden lift, and she lay bathed in peace as the light disappeared through the wall.

An angel? Have I encountered one of God's ministering angels? Or is this the death angel preparing me? Fear wanted to have the upper hand before a comforting thought replaced the fear. *Maybe God is showing me how much He cares about us, His children!* The afterglow stayed in their room a long time, and Michelle felt wrapped in its light.

"God is light, and in Him is no darkness at all," God's Word spoke to her.

Yes! God was light! When Donny would leave this world, he would be in the light of Jesus! Knowing the depth of Donny's relationship with Jesus Christ made heaven seem close. Knowing they would lose Donny was what caused her sorrow.

The next morning when Gail learned of his wife's experience, he said, "Don't fear. It may have been the death angel. I think God is preparing us, especially you," and he tenderly drew her close.

Michelle knew what her husband referred to. She did not want God to take Donny home to heaven. She longed for God to miraculously heal Donny and send him home a strong, healthy man so that Nicole would continue to have a caring husband and the boys would have a daddy.

But God was telling her otherwise. She knew God wanted to prepare her so that she could help her sister.

"Gail, this verse in Hebrews thrills my soul!" Michelle told him as she was reading her Bible that morning. "It's talking about angels, and it says, 'Are they not all ministering spirits, sent forth to minister for them who shall be heirs of salvation?' It verifies to me that God in His great love saw my need and sent His 'ministering spirit' to prepare and comfort me."

When Michelle shared her nighttime experience with Nicole and Danny, both of them asked each other the same questions.

"Do you think it was the death angel?"

"Is God preparing us?"

Donny privately bared his heart to his Lord as he wrote.

"O Lord, our, Lord, how excellent is thy name in all the earth!" When you bring people into my life who are hungry for any thread of hope, and you give me the opportunity to share your healing touch and the hope of Jesus Christ, my soul is thrilled! There is no greater hope I can offer than that of our ultimate healing.

"Lord, none of us know what is in store for us. My heart's desire is to be an instrument of hope to others going through difficult times. I weep for these people! Lord, as I pray with them, may your Word penetrate their hearts and take root. I long for each of them to have the assurance that the blood of Jesus covers their sins, so when they stand before you, they will hear the words: 'Your sins are forgiven! Enter into the joy of your Lord!'

"Send seeking souls, Lord. Send hurting souls. Send the unlovable. Oh, Lord my God, I am filled with a burning desire to help and encourage each cancer patient. Is this my life's work? Is this what you have for me to do before I leave this place? Lord, I am yours. Use me."

> *Choose my path, O blessed Saviour,*
> *Let me, trusting, lean on thee . . .*
> *Order thou my steps, dear Saviour,*
> *Just as seemeth good to thee.[1]*

To his family and friends he publicly shared:

Am I accepting the "training" in my life?

Picture with me a professional athlete preparing for a big event. He knows he must prepare himself so he can be strong and competitive. He has hopes of being the victor!

His coach paces him through grueling exercises and training. His body is strained to the maximum. Yet, through all this, the athlete never gets angry with his coach because he knows his coach has the best intentions in mind for him. He trusts that the coach wants him to be the winner. He knows that if he doesn't endure the pain of training now, his body will never adapt and become strong enough to compete in the real event.

---

[1] Ida L. Reed, public domain.

So we, too, must accept the training in our lives. We have a heavenly Father who knows what is best for us. He sees the future that we cannot see. He knows just what it will take to prepare us for what lies ahead.

So, we have a choice. We can become angry with our "Coach" for all the training we must go through, or we can put our trust in Him and have faith that He knows what is best!

"That the trial of your faith, being much more precious than of gold that perisheth, though it be tried with fire, might be found unto praise and honour and glory at the appearing of Jesus Christ" (1 Peter 1:7).

This past week has been a hefty training exercise for me, a very trying and tough week on my family. I have been having reactions to the treatments in the form of chills, fevers, and shakes. Once, Nicole found my pillow dripping with sweat. I had sweated most of the fluids out of my body. We think it was because of the pill I took to bring down my fever.

These times are so hard on Nicole. The boys, too, are so distraught at having Daddy sick and staying at the clinic. "Is Daddy going to be sick again and die?" You can see the fear written on Dallas's face.

"No, no! I don't want them to poke Daddy with a needle!" Dustin cried when the nurses were coming in to take my vital signs every fifteen minutes or so.

How do we comfort our children when we have the same questions?

God, in all His love and mercy, showed us by a good surprise that He was with us. Totally unexpectedly, our dear friends Delbert and Melissa Derstine ended up spending most of the week with us.

Melissa had come for a week of treatments, but things did not work out as planned, and they ended up not doing the treatments. They were discouraged when their plans did not work out, but when I started having reactions, they decided to spend the rest of their time with us. They not only gave us a moral and spiritual lift, but they were a big help with the boys while Nicole took care of me. We were sad to see them leave. "Thank you, God, for friends. You are so good!"

My blood test results are not looking very good, but we want to let my body rest. My immune system is so fragile that we do not want to do anything to cause more reactions.

On Monday I had a low-grade fever and did not sleep well. Tuesday evening I started feeling chills, and discouragement hit me with a blast.

"Lord, how long?" I cried in despair. Before I was even finished with the cry, I knew I needed to go to God in prayer. That was the only way. We put the boys to bed. Then Danny, Nicole, and I sat in a circle reading these commanding words of life:

> And Jesus answering saith unto them, Have faith
> in God. For verily I say into you, That whosoever
> shall say unto this mountain, Be thou removed,

and be thou cast into the sea; and shall not doubt in his heart, but shall believe that those things which he saith shall come to pass; he shall have whatsoever he saith. Therefore I say unto you, What things so ever ye desire, when ye pray, believe that ye receive them, and ye shall have them (Mark 11: 22–24).

Our desire was that God would take the fever away and that I would get a good night's rest. So we prayed in faith, believing. As we prayed, sweat began to form on my brow and run down my chest.

By the time we had finished praying, the fever had broken and my temperature was returning to normal. I went to bed and slept like a baby. In the morning I woke feeling refreshed. "Thank you, my Lord and my God, for answered prayer."

A few days after Donny sent the email his health took a bigger nosedive.

"Michelle?" Nicole's voice sounded so far away that they both keenly felt the agonizing distance between them. "Donny is having leg cramps again. It is like it was in the hospital in Columbus. Nothing helps. They have been going on the last couple days and nights. He even sits on the shower floor for hours, soaking up the warm water, but nothing helps."

That Saturday Gail and Michelle went looking for another van. They still hadn't gotten a replacement for the stolen one, and they felt God urging them to buy one NOW. *How soon will we need to go to Mexico?* The unspoken question hung over them.

"Gail, I've been praying while you were talking to the salesman," Michelle said as he shut the car door and reached for the key. "See that van over there?" she pointed. "Do you think it might be the one God wants us to get? I have a feeling we are going to need to leave for Mexico soon."

"No, I didn't see that van before, but I do like the looks of it," Gail said. As they checked things out, it seemed this was the van God was leading them to buy.

Several days after they had purchased the van, the phone rang. It was Donny. "Do you think you and Gail can come?" Donny begged Michelle. "I have pneumonia, and Nicole needs you."

With a heavy heart, Michelle called her husband at work. "Sweetheart, this is the end. Donny called and begged us to come. He has never done that before."

Donny sent one last email on May 1, 2010. He wrote:

I cannot write much. I am back in the clinic with a sharp pain in my left lung. The X-ray showed I have pneumonia in the bottom of the lung. The pain is so bad I have not slept the last three nights.

We had a huge surprise this morning. Gail, Michelle, and family walked through the door. Twenty-two hours from Oregon to give us support! Oh, the love of family!

Pray for Nicole, as this is wearing on her. Pray for our two precious boys, as they look so scared when they see Daddy like this. It feels like, *How much more can happen? How much more can we take?* I know if God wills, He has the power to heal, and so as long as I have life, I say as King David said: "I shall not die, but live, and declare the works of the Lord" (Psalm 118:17).

Gail and Michelle were not prepared for the shock they received upon entering Donny's hospital room. Dull eyes looked back at them out of a gaunt face. Gail went to Donny, and the men held each other's hands and cried. When Michelle took Donny's hand, he weakly cried out, "Oh, Michelle," and then looked down as he fought with deep emotion.

That evening while the other adults talked together, Danny entertained the children and watched them as they played on the hospital's flat rooftop. Donny was on oxygen, but he could still talk, and he shared his dream with Gail, Michelle, and Nicole, who were gathered around him. "I want to move down here and help hurting cancer patients. I want to continue the work God called me to do. I want to tell people what God can do for them, and what He has done for me.

"After all I have gone through, I don't feel I could go back to the normal lifestyle of working, sleeping, eating, and going to church—the continuous cycle," he confessed.

"Not that it is wrong—it isn't. I just feel God has something else for me."

Gail and Michelle listened, their hearts breaking. *Yes, Donny,* they wanted to cry out, *God has something far better waiting for you. He has heaven!*

"Stay with us tonight; I'm scared to be alone," Donny pleaded, so Gail stayed. Donny would drift off to sleep, jerk awake, and then do it all over again. He tried to talk, but it was hard for him to breathe. "I—feel—like—I—am—falling," he would stammer out with great effort. Then he would relax when he saw Gail sitting on the bed.

Gail experienced his own heartbreak as he sat on the end of his best friend's bed, watching him endure excruciating pain yet unable to do anything. The only thing he could think to do was to sing. So he sang.

One time he asked Donny if he had a favorite song. Donny replied, "Saviour, Like a Shepherd Lead Us." Through the dark hours, the dying man heard heavenly music sung from the lips of his friend and brother-in-law. Nicole fell asleep, but Gail sang on. Donny drifted in and out of sleep, but with God's enabling strength, Gail sang praise after praise in that dark, lonely, pain-filled night.

Weird lumps would appear on one side of Donny's neck, and then disappear and appear on the other side. By morning, Donny needed continuous oxygen. His legs were filling with fluid, and an X-ray showed his lungs filling also.

Bruce Northy from the Oasis clinic stopped in to visit Donny, and one glance at his friend caused him to cry.

When Bruce left the room, he found Nicole coming down the hall and told her, "Nicole, your husband has done a beautiful work here. I love listening to him encourage other people and share the plan of salvation and his testimony for God. That's why I have had him share in chapel when he can. He is dealing with so much suffering himself. He understands the needs of the ones he ministers to. That is why people gravitate to him. They know he understands. They know he is real because they see him battling pain, fevers, nausea, and weakness, but he never complains!

"Instead, he testifies of God's goodness. He shares about how God offers complete healing to everyone through the cleansing of sinful hearts washed clean by Jesus Christ.

"I've heard him and Danny sing many times, and I have seen how others were moved and encouraged. They realized they were not struggling alone. A person sees and feels the love of God within him.

"I want you to know I love Donny. He touched my life." And with that, Bruce left, wiping tears that would not stop.

Alma, Donny's "Mexican Mama," came into his room and took his thin hand in both of hers. "Oh, my son, my son!" she cried with tears in her eyes. It was so amazing to Nicole to see Alma's hardened, uncaring mask fall away when she was in Donny's presence.

That evening the two couples were eating together in Donny's room when Donny looked at Michelle and said, "Michelle, I am so tired."

Not knowing what he meant, she asked, "Do you want

us to leave so you can sleep?"

"No," he responded, "I am tired of fighting." Tears came into his eyes.

Nicole looked at her sister, and they knew the end was near. The room became deathly quiet as each of them felt the strangling impact of his words. Gail went over to Donny and held him in his arms, both of them crying. Then Gail and Michelle quietly left the room so that Nicole could be alone with the love of her life.

Nicole crawled up on the hospital bed next to her husband and laid her head on his shoulder for the last time, sobbing into his weak arms. Both of them were crying, and because Donny was on oxygen, he could only talk in a whisper.

"I don't understand. I never thought God would take me like this. Oh, God, why?" he cried softly. Then in a soft voice Nicole heard him say, "Help me, Lord. I am so tired. Please help me."

Nicole gently clung to her husband and told him, "Darling, I have never regretted marrying you. I have treasured every moment together. God will see us through this."

Calmness filled her heart. Though tears rolled down her face, she assured him, "Donny, God has been with me through all the hardships of the last four and a half years. I know God will be with me through this too." She could see the comfort her testimony brought to her husband as he absorbed her words.

Her husband had always been the strong one, and now

she needed to be the stronger of the two. In these moments, the last that they would have alone together, Nicole found her suffering husband leaning on her.

Gail, Michelle, and Danny returned, and together they laid their hands on Donny and prayed. Joy shot through Nicole as she heard her husband praying. Each word took great effort, but the beauty of his prayer riveted on the hearts of the ones gathered around his bedside.

"My—Lord, I—had asked—that—you—heal—me. I—wanted—to serve—you. My—life—is yours. Take—me, use—me. I'll—go—where—you—want—me—to—go."

Each one leaned close to catch his words. When Donny finished, he lay still with his eyes closed as he focused on breathing.

"Why don't I stay with you tonight?" Danny suggested to Nicole. "Then Gail can sleep." The exhausted young wife thought she could not bear the endless night filled with strangled breathing as her loved one struggled for each breath. She found it extremely difficult to watch her husband, reduced to skin and bones, fighting to breathe with the help of oxygen, but Nicole did not complain. Lovingly she tended to her husband's needs. Danny helped her change the cold cloths they wrapped around Donny's feet to try to bring down the fever and give some comfort.

The next morning Michelle met her sister waiting for them in the hall. Nicole fell into her arms, sobbing her heart out. Her face had a haunted stare, and there were dark circles under her eyes. All Michelle had time to do was put her arms around her before Dr. Tony arrived to talk to Donny.

"Donny, you are in serious condition. We need to move you over to Oasis where they are better equipped for your needs. You need to have the fluid siphoned off your lungs so you can breathe. They will use a needle to do the procedure. It is somewhat risky, but there is no alternative," the doctor explained to his patient.

"Did—we—make—a—mistake—in—pulling—out—the—tooth?" Donny asked him.

"We did what we thought we should. We thought we were going to beat it," Dr. Tony answered as he stood and put his hand on Donny to give comfort. Nicole laid her head on her husband's lap, sobbing.

"I—don't—know—why," Donny labored to answer, and Michelle put her arms around them both.

"We have to lean on God," she encouraged as she cried with them. *Please Lord, give each of us the strength to go through what is ahead,* she pleaded inwardly.

Donny was moved to Oasis. They all knew time was running out. Gail and Michelle took the children down to the cafeteria for supper. Nicole leaned down and gave her husband a kiss. He stared up into her eyes.

How long, Lord? she wondered. *It is so hard! I want him to be healed. But Lord, you will heal him! He will never suffer again when you give him your ultimate healing touch. Your will be done.* She held his hand, willing him to feel the peace in her heart. The children came back upstairs with popsicles, but Dustin did not want to finish his.

"Daddy can have it," he offered. Donny took it with a smile carving his sunken cheeks. He sucked on it a little. Pain exploded in Nicole's chest. *Our boys! Oh, Lord, is this the last time they will see Daddy smile?*

Donny could not breathe while lying down, so Gail pushed the end table up to the end of the bed and helped him lean forward onto a pillow. The plans to have fluid removed changed when a specialist came into Donny's room and informed them he was convinced the trouble was not the fluid but the pneumonia.

"There is too much risk involved in taking off the little fluid there is. I recommend a strong antibiotic to combat the pneumonia. Pound his back like this." The doctor showed Nicole. "It will help to break up the mucus."

Not long after the doctor left, Donny began having more trouble breathing, and his oxygen saturation level began dropping.

"Sing—'Saviour—Like—a Shepherd—Lead—Us,'" he requested.

Danny and Gail stood at the end of the bed and sang.

> *Saviour, like a shepherd lead us,*
> *Much we need thy tend'rest care . . .*
> *We are thine, do thou befriend us,*
> *Be the guardian of our way . . .*
> *Thou hast promised to receive us,*
> *Poor and sinful tho' we be . . .*

Blessed Jesus! Blessed Jesus!
Thou hast loved us, love us still.[2]

. . . .

Swish, swish. The oxygen machine seemed to fill the room with its steady rhythm, a stark reminder of reality. Yet as they stood around Donny, the room was not depressing. Instead, it seemed hallowed, filled with God's peaceful presence.

Donny relaxed for a moment after they finished singing. Then he moved restlessly.

"What's wrong?" Nicole asked as he grew agitated and changed positions.

"I—need—more—air," the faint answer came as barely a whisper. Nicole checked the oxygen regulator on the wall.

"Love! I can't turn it any higher!" Her eyes widened as she looked at her brother- in-law and cousin. Once more Donny asked for air. They could see his oxygen saturation level dropping on the monitor. Nicole ran for the doctor and returned staggering, white as a sheet and ready to collapse. Gail helped her into the chair by the bed.

There was nothing the doctors and nurses could do. "I love you," Nicole cried and held her husband.

"I—love—you," Donny returned. He leaned back on the bed, took another breath, and slipped away to meet his Maker. Donny's fight was over. His earthly battle had

---

[2] Dorothy A. Thrupp, public domain.

ceased, and he was lifted into the arms of Jesus.

In all, Donny had spent seventy-eight weeks in Mexico ministering to other hurting individuals before God said, "Donny, your work is finished. I have come to release a faithful, weary soldier from duty."

Michelle was at the motel with all the children when Donny passed away, so Gail sent her a text to let her know what had happened. Donny's body was soon taken from Oasis, and Danny and Gail took Nicole back to the motel. Michelle found her sister in the throes of shock and agony, unaware of what she was doing. When Nicole sat down on the stairs, Michelle gently helped her to bed and covered her with a blanket. Then Michelle kept silent vigil beside her as Nicole slept fitfully through the dark morning.

When Dallas and Dustin awoke, Nicole was still sleeping, and Gail and Michelle knew it was up to them to tell the boys. With tears running down their faces, they held the two fatherless boys on their laps and explained, "Daddy went to be with Jesus last night. He isn't sick anymore, because he is in heaven with Jesus."

Big, blue eyes stared up into theirs, and the little boys looked at each other before Dallas solemnly said, "My mommy is a widow now." Their hearts broke as Dustin mimicked, "Mommy is a widow now."

"Yes," Michelle answered as she wrapped her arms around both boys. "Mommy misses Daddy, and you boys do too. It's okay to cry," she assured, and Dallas burst out crying—great, wrenching sobs. Gail and Michelle did not know what to do but hold the boys close, little boys who knew so much about dying. Because Dallas was crying, Dustin started crying too.

The boys had sat many times with their parents at the bedside of dying patients. They had listened while their daddy and mommy had sung to, prayed for, and comforted sick, grieving people. Often Daddy had explained to them how much Jesus loved everyone, and what a wonderful, beautiful place heaven was. Dallas knew no one was sick in heaven, but if Daddy was in heaven, how could he see him?

That morning Gail sent the following email:

> *Dear Friends and Family,*
>
> *Donny's earthly journey did not end in defeat, but in victory on Wednesday, May 5, at 2 a.m. Not victory over the disease that racked his body for four and a half years, but victory over death. Donny always said he would be healed, and he fought with all he had to become well and continue to serve his Lord. His determination, courage, and resourcefulness were an example to many. He often found ways to help others on their journeys of physical and spiritual sickness.*
>
> *We know Donny is healed because God's Word tells us that there is no sickness, pain, or death in heaven. Although Donny felt he had a mission on earth to fill, and he did not want to leave, he was ready to meet his Maker and Judge. Will each of us be ready when it is our time to go?*

Both sets of parents arrived in Mexico that same Wednesday morning. By Thursday evening, Donny's body was released to go to the United States. Danny, along with Gail and Michelle and their family, left that evening to drive straight home, and the others flew to Oregon the next day.

Because the Porter Mennonite Church building could not accommodate a large crowd, the funeral was held at the Estacada First Baptist Church. Tuesday, May 11, 2010, dawned with heavy, overcast skies. No warming sunbeams filtered through the heavy pines to dispel the morning's chill. It seemed to the people arriving for the 10:00 funeral service that even the heavens were sorrowing with them.

Nicole felt God walking with her. His abiding presence sustained her. In the midst of overwhelming grief, an aura of peace radiated from the sorrowing mother. The boys reflected her calmness by being content to sit quietly on her lap or beside her. Later, she testified, "Without God, it would have been impossible to endure that day."

"What is life?" Nolan Bechtel challenged each person in the audience as he began the funeral message. "I want to use four points from the Word of God that define life.

"Life is a gift from God, a precious gift that is loaned to us. Life is an opportunity to believe the Word of God. Life is an opportunity to experience the Word in our hearts, and life is an opportunity to do the will of God." He expounded further on those points before asking the question, "What is death? The Bible tells us that out of death comes something better.

"Death can be the gateway to a beautiful life with God. The body, at the resurrection, is raised in glory. Death is not the end. For those who know God, death is the beginning of eternal life. But to those who do not know God, it is the beginning of eternal dying. Death can be a precious thing. 'Precious in the sight of the Lord is the death of his saints.'

"Donny's life was short but rich. He was enthusiastic about life. Whatever he did, he did with all he had. Whether in working, public speaking, witnessing, or finding a way to live, Donny did it 100 percent. Donny wanted to live, but with that desire was a desire to glorify his Maker."

Nolan concluded his message with the reminder, "The tears today are our tears. They are not Donny's. And God has given us the promise: 'Joy cometh in the morning.' May God bless each of you."

After the message, Danny led a quartet in singing several favorite songs that Donny and he had sung in the hospital and clinics together. Then there was a time of sharing about Donny's life.

Dr. Tony Jimenez from Mexico went forward and gave testimony to Donny's personal work in his clinic. "Donny was a Christ-fearing young man who taught me many things. How did he affect my faith? I cannot put it in words, but my focus has shifted in many ways because of the impact of Donny's life. I also bring greetings from my staff. Donny touched everyone. My assisting staff physician, Alma in administration, Gloria, Anna, and even my wife, who has never met Donny and Nicole but has prayed a lot for the family—all of them say, 'We love you, Nicole, Dallas, and Dustin.' And remember, Nicole, choose to live."

After Dr. Tony sat down, several others went forward to share reflections. Edwin Bontrager told the audience, "Donny endeavored to see God clearly in all circumstances. He was compassionate to those in need. He fought valiantly. God blessed him with a woman of strength, who walked by his side and comforted him."

Then a gentleman, not known to the family or anyone else there, walked to the podium. "I probably know Donny less than anyone else here," he began. "The day I met Donny, I was wearing a red heart sticker on my jacket that said, 'I gave blood today.'

" 'So you gave blood today?' Donny asked me.

" 'Yes, I did,' I answered. 'I came from Portland, and I gave platelets.'

" 'Thank you for saving my life,' Donny told me. 'I received blood eight times, and it has helped to get me to where I am. I'm in remission from cancer.'

" 'You're welcome,' I replied, and in that brief instant, for about ten seconds, our eyes and hearts met. I have never forgotten Donny. Today, his struggles are over. I read his obituary in the newspaper, and I had to come."

"Donny and Nicole lived in my sister's trailer, about

fifty yards from our house," Elton Miller shared. "In the three years they lived there, I never heard him complain. When they would return from treatments, we would not see them much because Donny never felt good when they first returned. If I would stop in and ask him how things were going, he would answer simply, 'I have fevers, etc.,' but he always spoke as if he were talking about someone else, not himself. He would smile his famous smile and change the subject to something I was connected with. In the past week when Donny was fighting his last battle, I walked over to the flowerbed they had planted earlier, and I saw one lone, red tulip holding its head high. The tulip seemed to be proclaiming, 'I am paying tribute to Donny's efforts.' I have been blessed by Donny's cheerful determination to bloom where God planted him."

"I, too, am thankful I could be a part of Donny's life." Gail paused to gain control of his emotions. "We grew up together in Ohio, and for almost eight years I have been privileged to know him as a brother-in-law. Donny and I would often drive by Mt. Hood, and Donny would say, 'Let's climb it someday!' We never did climb it, but when God gave him another mountain to climb, Donny did not say, 'I want something more glamorous.' Instead, he climbed his mountain, with determination, to the very top."

Another friend related, "I have been inspired by Donny's zest for life. In every prayer I heard Donny pray, he would always thank God for life. It has made me aware of how precious the gift of life is."

The last young man who took the stand shared this. "I didn't know Donny very well, but his faithfulness to God challenged me. We were holding street meetings in Portland, and you could see that Donny was not ashamed to be identified with God. I heard a minister say, 'When you die, don't leave any question marks.' There is no question in our minds where Donny is today. He lived an open and pure life. He was a humble person. Because of Jesus, Donny's testimony will live on."

Tears flowed that day, tears of sorrow for those remaining, but also tears of rejoicing that Donny, their friend and loved one, was free from earthly suffering and was now experiencing the everlasting "joy of the Lord."

DADDY, ARE YOU SAD?

20

Donny's Family's Journey

In the weeks and months that followed Donny's death, Nicole found it healing to keep in contact with friends via email. The updates she sent told of the journey that she and her children were experiencing as they adjusted to life without Donny.

June 2010 – It has been six weeks since my dear, sweet husband passed from this earth. They have been six weeks of sorrow, loneliness, and utter agony, but through it all I still can say that God has given me a peace and strength I would not have thought possible.

The boys and I moved into one of the bedrooms at Gail and Michelle's home. Even though it was crowded, we had "our own little spot" where we could shut the door and be a family.

When our friends, Melissa and Delbert Derstine from North Carolina, came out to Oregon for Donny's funeral, the Lord laid it on my heart to offer to go lend help and support to Melissa. By that time her cancer had metasta-sized to the bones and lung.

God also spoke to Danny's heart, and he felt he should go with me and help Delbert with his work. We had planned to wait three to six weeks before going, but plans changed when Melissa got home and took a turn for the worse. Four days after Donny's funeral we were on our way to North Carolina.

August 2010 – Melissa is now with her Lord. The past three and a half months, I stayed with her and her family, and it has been a very important part of my healing journey. She was there for me in my darkest hours, a lighthouse during a raging storm. Reaching out to help and love her was a healing balm to my broken heart.

October 2010 – We are on a trip to Missouri with Donny's brother Jerry and his wife Melrose. We are attending the wedding of Sam Eigsti, a widower with seven children. You may remember Donny writing about Sam, as he paid us a surprise visit while we were at the clinic.

From Missouri we will go on to visit Donny's parents in Ohio. Then we will return to Oregon. Once again we will be living at my sister's place.

As Nicole typed that email, she asked herself. *Am I never to have a home to call my own? Will my "things" forever be in storage?*

October 12 dawned a gray, sunless morning that matched the dreariness within Nicole's heart. Today would have been their eighth anniversary. Before the boys awoke, she sought solace from God, seeking strength to be cheerful.

The day seemed long, and in her restlessness she wrote another letter to her scattered friends.

October 12, 2010 – Today we would have celebrated eight years of marriage. Half of them were filled with suffering and sorrow. I am so thankful that, in spite of the cross we had to carry, we were blessed with a happy, close relationship. It is hard to face the future alone, without Donny, but God has promised a lamp for our feet, not a crystal ball that allows us to see into our future. I do not need to know what will happen tomorrow. I only need to believe He leads us, and we will "find grace to help in time of need."

In November Nicole shared:

November 2010 – One thing that keeps me going is my strong desire not to disappoint my dear husband. This helps me in my struggle not to be bitter, to keep reaching out to those who are hurting, and to look past my own pain to testify to the world of God's unceasing presence and strength through the darkest waters. Donny touched and changed so many lives. Mine is one of them.

One question I'm plagued with is, "Who am I?" In the last five years I have had the health of my husband, our home, money, things, and then my husband himself, taken away. My question to myself is, "Am I truly what God wants me to be?"

You really find out what kind of person you are when you have almost everything taken away. So my solution has been to clean out my closets spiritually and, with God's help, rid myself of my besetting sins—stubbornness and willfulness. My strong will has, in some ways, helped me through the last years, but it has also caused me problems.

I am also getting rid of anything that has been too important to me—any material idols. I'm determined to have nothing stand between God and me. I want nothing to hinder God's work in me, lest these trials I have gone through be in vain. To be totally broken and submitted to His will is what God asks of me and what I am striving toward. My heavenly Father is ever patient and loving!

Before Christmas she wrote the final letter for 2010.

December 2010 – I read a poem that says: "I had my first Christmas in heaven." I could just hear Donny saying, "Here's my greeting! Look up, dear ones, till that day appears! What a Christmas is waiting for you!"

I had to think what perfect bliss he must be experiencing! How we miss him, but how can I wish him back to a pain- and sorrow-filled life? All we can do is be ready to meet him some day. I CAN'T WAIT!

"Thank you, God, for sending your Son. Because of this, we have the hope of seeing our loved ones again!"

Nicole couldn't stop smiling. As soon as the boys were sleeping, she opened her computer and typed excitedly.

January 15, 2011 – Many times in the past five years I have had the privilege to experience firsthand the miracles God performed on our behalf: answered prayers, money provided right when it was needed, and a clear sense of His presence in the low times. But there is nothing like a reminder that God is walking by my side to assure me that I have nothing to fear!

A miracle happened to me today. I went to the dentist because of increasing nerve pain in one of my teeth. All said and done, the bill to fix it would have been almost one thousand dollars! I was feeling blue and discouraged.

"Lord," I said, "either I will end up being a happy widow with no teeth, or you will have to provide the funds." I drove home, walked in the door, and found one piece of mail on the table for me. I opened it to find a check for one thousand dollars!

Amazing! "Thank you, Jesus!"

Nicole's next correspondence began:

My dear friends! I hope you don't get tired of hearing from me. But tonight I do want to tell you what I experienced today. I call it joy in the midst of sorrow.

Loneliness. Decisions. The future. All of these turned my tears on, and Dustin came running to where I sat. Crawling onto my lap, he asked, "What's wrong, Mommy?"

"I'm just missing Daddy," I said, wiping the tears that persisted in coming.

Reaching up, he took both of his little three-year-old hands and cupped my face, saying, "Don't cry, Mommy. I love you." Then he pressed his face against mine. Without saying another word, he got down, and bringing some toys, he climbed back on my lap. He sat for about an hour playing with his toys, but every so often he would look up into my face. If he thought I needed love, he would press his sweet face against mine before returning to play.

What would I do without my dear little boys?

Ten months had passed since Donny left a widow and two small boys to face life alone. Yet they were not alone. Nicole had reached out to many people in those ten long months, and in doing so she had taken up the work Donny had started of ministering to others.

Nicole sent another email in March of 2011.

I have been in Squaw Valley, California, for three weeks now with my dear friend Miriam.

She has five children and is a fellow sojourner through grief and sorrow. We first met at the Rubio Center when her husband Vernon came for treatments. Three years ago he passed on to his heavenly home after complications from an infection.

I have needed and appreciated the support I have gotten from all my friends and family, but there are times you feel like you are going crazy by being surrounded with couples! Only another person who has walked through the valley of grief comprehends what it is like to lose your mate. It has been therapeutic here for my boys to talk with other fatherless children. Miriam and I heard them talking about what their daddies were doing up in heaven together.

"Dallas, who are you talking to?" Nicole asked one day when she entered his room and saw he was alone.

"I'm talking to Daddy," he answered.

Nicole remembered the time in Mexico when Dallas had asked his father, "Daddy, are you sad?" and she thought of that now as Dallas tilted his head toward the ceiling in the direction of heaven where his father now lived.

As she watched him, it was as if she could hear Donny's reply to that question Dallas had asked him. *No, son, there is no sadness in heaven where I am! My heart does not hurt. I am with Jesus! There is no pain in heaven!*

And son, you should see the streets of shining gold I walk on. And the river! It is clear as crystal. I will be waiting to meet you when you enter the gates of this heavenly city. My son, you cannot hold your daddy's hand, but you can hold tight to the hand of Jesus. Do this, and someday we will all be together forever and ever.

The young widow's eyes were wet as the unspoken message washed over her—a message she knew her husband would have spoken. She reached for her son and gave him a hug. "You can talk to Daddy anytime you want," she assured him. "Or you can talk to Jesus. He always hears us and wants us to talk to Him."

Epilogue

Only one week after Donny's funeral, Nicole and the boys were kneeling beside the bed saying their bedtime prayers.

"Thank you for my good daddy in heaven," Dallas prayed. "And I pray that you would send us a new good daddy. Amen." Shock waves coursed through Nicole, sending a chill she could not shake. *It's just over a week since we buried Donny!* She wanted to lash out, to stop her son's plea. But night after night, month after month, her persistent little boy ended his bedtime prayer with the same request.

. . . .

The December 1, 2011, deadline to sign up for the winter Los Angeles street meetings was just a few days away. Nicole found herself in the throes of indecision. Should she go help in these meetings sponsored by their church and other churches in the West? Or was her responsibility at home with her boys?

"Lord," she prayed earnestly, "the deadline is almost here. I need to send in my application if I want to go, but is it right to leave my boys for a week? I want to go, but am I being selfish? I feel like I'm doing so little for you, Lord!

Homeschooling keeps me so busy. I know it is well worth the effort, but isn't there something else for me? Lord, I want to be doing more for you!" The challenge of intense witnessing for Christ on the teeming streets of Los Angeles tugged harder at her heart and would not let her rest.

"Nicole," Michelle reminded her, "it's not like you are leaving your boys with strangers. You know our home is basically your home. Yes, you sleep and do school work over in your little travel trailer, but you do live with us! The boys will love sleeping here and be just fine!"

. . . .

While Nicole Good filled out her application for the Los Angeles street meetings, Darwin Eby from Maryland was also struggling with whether he, too, should help with the work in Los Angeles. *I've been going for years! I'm thirty-five years old. Is this all you have for me, Lord? Am I never to experience the blessings of married life?* his heart asked God.

"Go to Los Angeles," God's spirit prompted. Darwin obeyed, and as he prepared to leave on the mission trip, he felt God clearly telling him, "Darwin, I do know your heart's desire and your prayer. I do have someone for you, but you need to go to Los Angeles."

Darwin Eby traveled to the West Coast under God's divine direction. Nicole Good joined the team under the same divine direction. Two individuals, doing the will of the Father, met for the first time, and in that meeting, both experienced a profound realization that it was God directing their path.

. . . .

On February 18, 2012, Nicole sent the following email to friends.

Ecclesiastes 3:1, 4, and 8 say, "To everything there is a season, and a time to every purpose under the heaven: A time to weep, and a time to laugh; a time to mourn, and a time to dance; a time to love . . ."

My life has taken a new path, one filled with renewed hope and love! God has worked a miracle, and the boys' faith-filled prayers of the last nineteen months are being answered!

My family is very happy, and though the pain and grief of losing Donny is still there for all of us, Darwin has been welcomed with love and open arms.

To everything there is a season, and a time to every purpose under heaven. Ecclesiastes 3:1

Rejoicing in God's leading in our lives, we,

Nicole Adiel Good

and

Darwin Ray Eby

together with our families, invite you to celebrate with us as we join our lives as one on Saturday, the seventh of July Two thousand and twelve at ten o'clock in the morning Estacada First Baptist Church Estacada, Oregon

A time to weep, and a time to laugh, a time to mourn, and a time to dance. Ecclesiastes 3:4

. . . .

Seven months later on July 7, 2012, two excited little boys entered the Estacada First Baptist Church. "Today we are getting married!" they exclaimed. To them it meant, "Today we are getting a daddy!"

Tears were shed as friends and loved ones shared in the joy of two little beaming faces watching Mommy and their new daddy exchange marriage vows.

"Before we kneel to pray, I have another question," Bishop Edwin Bontrager announced. Turning to Darwin he asked, "Do you promise to raise these two boys as your own?"

"I do," came the clear unwavering reply. It echoed throughout the church's stillness and into every recess of Nicole's uplifted heart.

Darwin and Nicole Eby and family in 2013, including newborn son Cedric Darwin.

Life Is Like a Rose

Do you ever think about how life is like a rose offered to us by God?

You see, God doesn't just give me the soft beautiful petals off the rose. Instead He offers to me the whole rose, stem and all. As God extends to me this beautiful rose, I have a choice. I can either reject the rose because I'm too afraid of the thorns that may cause me pain, or I can accept the rose and reach out for the thorn-covered stem.

As I take hold of the rose and clasp my hands around the stem, the thorns pierce my hand . . . oh, the pain! But the longer I hold the rose, the more I begin to discover the beauty of it. And as I discover the beauty of it, it lessens the pain of the thorn piercing my hand. I begin to accept the thorns; I can intertwine my fingers among them so the pain is not so bad.

As I hold the rose of my life, my hand holds and covers the thorns. But those around me see a beautiful flower. With confidence I can hold up the rose of my life, that others may see and smell the lovely fragrance that flows from it, seeing the beautiful work God is doing in my life.

My friend . . . what are you doing with the rose God is offering you?

"Then shall the righteous shine forth as the sun in the kingdom of their Father" (Matthew 13: 43a).

—Donny Good

About the Author

Lily Bear lives with her husband David on a grain farm in northwestern Ohio. During forty years of marriage, God has blessed them with five children and fourteen grandchildren.

Born in northern Alberta to a story-telling father, she had an early love for books and writing. But Lily admits that writing is intense work. She is thankful for her husband, who supports her and prays for her. She is also grateful to God for directing her thoughts as she writes. It is her desire that this book would glorify Christ and Him alone.

If you wish to contact Lily, you may write to her in care of Christian Aid Ministries, P.O. Box 360, Berlin, Ohio 44610.

Christian Aid Ministries

Christian Aid Ministries was founded in 1981 as a non-profit, tax-exempt 501(c)(3) organization. Its primary purpose is to provide a trustworthy and efficient channel for Amish, Mennonite, and other conservative Anabaptist groups and individuals to minister to physical and spiritual needs around the world. This is in response to the command ". . . do good unto all men, especially unto them who are of the household of faith" (Galatians 6:10).

Each year, CAM supporters provide approximately 15 million pounds of food, clothing, medicines, seeds, Bibles, Bible story books, and other Christian literature for needy people. Most of the aid goes to orphans and Christian families. Supporters' funds also help clean up and rebuild for natural disaster victims, put up Gospel billboards in the U.S., support several church-planting efforts, operate two medical clinics, and provide resources for needy families to make their own living. CAM's main purposes for providing aid are to help and encourage God's people and bring the Gospel to a lost and dying world.

CAM has staff, warehouse, and distribution networks in

Romania, Moldova, Ukraine, Haiti, Nicaragua, Liberia, and Israel. Aside from management, supervisory personnel, and bookkeeping operations, volunteers do most of the work at CAM locations. Each year, volunteers at our warehouses, field bases, DRS projects, and other locations donate over 200,000 hours of work.

CAM's ultimate purpose is to glorify God and help enlarge His kingdom. ". . . whatsoever ye do, do all to the glory of God" (1 Corinthians 10:31).

The Way to God
and Peace

We live in a world contaminated by sin. Sin is anything that goes against God's holy standards. When we do not follow the guidelines that God our Creator gave us, we are guilty of sin. Sin separates us from God, the source of life.

Since the time when the first man and woman, Adam and Eve, sinned in the Garden of Eden, sin has been universal. The Bible says that we all have "sinned and come short of the glory of God" (Romans 3:23). It also says that the natural consequence for that sin is eternal death, or punishment in an eternal hell: "Then when lust hath conceived, it bringeth forth sin: and sin, when it is finished, bringeth forth death" (James 1:15).

But we do not have to suffer eternal death in hell. God provided forgiveness for our sins through the death of His only Son, Jesus Christ. Because Jesus was perfect and without sin, He could die in our place. "For God so loved the world that he gave his only begotten Son, that whosoever believeth in him should not perish, but have everlasting life" (John 3:16).

A sacrifice is something given to benefit someone else. It costs the giver greatly. Jesus was God's sacrifice. Jesus' death takes away the penalty of sin for everyone who accepts this sacrifice and truly repents of their sins. To repent of sins means to be truly sorry for and turn away from the things we have done that have violated God's standards. (Acts 2:38; 3:19).

Jesus died, but He did not remain dead. After three days, God's Spirit miraculously raised Him to life again. God's Spirit does something similar in us. When we receive Jesus as our sacrifice and repent of our sins, our hearts are changed. We become spiritually alive! We develop new desires and attitudes (2 Corinthians 5:17). We begin to make choices that please God (1 John 3:9). If we do fail and commit sins, we can ask God for forgiveness. "If we confess our sins, he is faithful and just to forgive us our sins, and to cleanse us from all unrighteousness" (1 John 1:9).

Once our hearts have been changed, we want to continue growing spiritually. We will be happy to let Jesus be the Master of our lives and will want to become more like Him. To do this, we must meditate on God's Word and commune with God in prayer. We will testify to others of this change by being baptized and sharing the good news of God's victory over sin and death. Fellowship with a faithful group of believers will strengthen our walk with God (1 John 1:7).